The Histories

and

Prophecies

of

Daniel

The Histories and Prophecies of Daniel

Robert Duncan Culver

BMH Books
Winona Lake,
Indiana 46590

TO MY CHILDREN,
Douglas, Keith and Lorraine,
who heard most of this book first hand,
in company with their mother, at church and class,
before it was ever put together
in manuscript form for a book.

The Scripture references and quotations in this book are taken from the King James and the 1901 American Standard Versions of the Bible.

Cover design by Jane Fretz

ISBN: 0-88469-131-4

COPYRIGHT 1980
BMH BOOKS
WINONA LAKE, INDIANA

Printed in U.S.A.

Preface

To Daniel

① START INTRODUCTION

The times in which we live certainly dictate our interests; and these are troublous times. What is going to happen? Where are the leaders and nations headed? The books of prophecy that are found in the Scriptures give us the guidelines that are needed to provide the answers. The Book of Daniel is one of those wonderful gems that God has given to us. This book combines the beauty of history and prophecy, and gives examples of godly living.

To read about a young man dedicated to God and living in a nation foreign to him, has always been a source of inspiration to believers. To comprehend that God can empower a prophet, and then give wisdom, understanding, and protection to carry out the assigned mission, brings hope to those who follow God. One may have difficulty following the historical and prophetical references of this book, but one is never left with a feeling that God is not in full control of all circumstances.

Go to page 5 #2 book

Robert Duncan Culver does a fine piece of work in presenting this study commentary on the Book of Daniel. His background qualifies him well for the task. Having taught the Book of Daniel in classrooms many times, has helped Mr. Culver bring into focus the fine details of the book. His practical instruction in churches has also aided in the practical communication of the teaching of this outstanding Old Testament portion.

You will be challenged mentally with scriptural truths, and you will find enrichment for your spiritual life in the study of this writing. It has been prepared to be used for individual/private study, in adult Sunday school classes, and home Bible studies, as well as in Bible institutes and colleges.

Charles W. Turner

BMH Books
August 1980

Table of Contents

Preface 5

1. The Historical Background of the Book of Daniel: A Story of Moral Heroism (Dan., Chap. 1) 9
2. Nebuchadnezzar's Dream of a Great Image: A Prophecy of the "Times of the Gentiles" (Dan., Chap. 2) 25
3. Three Heroes in a Fiery Furnace: A Lesson in Steadfast Faith (Dan., Chap. 3) 45
4. The Dream of a High Tree: A Lesson in Humility (Dan., Chap. 4) 60
5. Belshazzar's Feast: A Lesson in Sin and Its Fruit (Dan., Chap. 5) 74
6. Daniel in the Lions' Den: A Message of Faith and Prayer (Dan., Chap. 6) 89
7. Four Beasts, the Ancient of Days, and the Son of Man: A Prophecy of Christ and Antichrist (Dan., Chap. 7) 103
8. A Ram, a Goat, and a Little Horn: Prophecy of Israel in Conflict with the Old Testament Antichrist (Dan., Chap. 8) 119
9. A Story of an Immediate Answer to Prayer (Dan., Chap. 9:1-23) 133
10. The Prophecy of the Seventy Weeks (Dan., Chap. 9:24-27) 147
11. A Vision of God: A Story of Delayed Answer to Prayer (Dan., Chaps. 10:1–11:35) 162
12. Summary of Old Testament Eschatology: Israel's Final Future in the Plan of God (Dan., Chaps. 11:36–12:13) 175

1

Daniel 1

The Historical Background of the Book of Daniel:

A Story of Moral Heroism

I. Circumstances Providing the Setting (Dan. 1:1-5)

II. The Identity of the Chief Actor and His Associates (Dan. 1:6-7)

III. Events Placing the Author in the Position He Holds throughout the Book (Dan. 1:5-20)

The historical narrative of the Book of Daniel relates mainly to events which transpired in or near the city of Babylon, located on the banks of the Euphrates about 400 miles due east of northern Palestine. The earliest events recorded took place in about the year 605 B.C. and the latest in about 534 B.C. All is reported by a man introduced at the beginning as a youth named Daniel and described at the close as a very aged man.

For helpful information on backgrounds to Daniel—the two languages in which it was written, history of the time, the special character of Daniel as the first biblical book of *Apocalypse* and other technical matters, the reader is referred to more technical works. See the present author's *Daniel and the Latter Days* (Moody Press, 1977) and his treatment of Daniel in *Wycliffe Commentary* (Moody Press, 1962).

The portion now under consideration, chapter 1, has a designed relation to the whole book. In it the historical setting is laid. We learn when and where these things happened. We are introduced to the chief actors. And, we learn how these particular people happened to be in focus at this time.

There is, however, a singularly valuable series of lessons in the moral heroism of the four Hebrew boys whose story is introduced here. This makes the chapter of great worth quite apart from the rest of the book.

In a day when the sports and entertainment world is furnishing our people, especially youth, with many very unworthy objects of emulation; this story about four of God's truly human heroes is sorely needed.

I. CIRCUMSTANCES PROVIDING THE SETTING
(Dan. 1:1-5)

1. The Time

In the third year of the reign of Jehoiakim king of Judah came Nebuchadnezzar king of Babylon unto Jerusalem, and besieged it (Dan. 1:1).

As recently as December 1956 were first published the archaeological findings which provide full support for Nebuchadnezzar's presence in Palestine and which make this capture of Jerusalem by the Babylonians in 605 B.C. credible even to skeptical historians.

Actually there were at least three occasions when Nebuchadnezzar's armies besieged Jerusalem. The present passage of Scripture relates the first. A second was in the year 597 B.C. in the first year of Jehoiachin when Nebuchadnezzar carried away King Jehoiachin. This was the time of the transportation of Ezekiel (see 2 Kings 24:8-16; Ezek. 1:1). The final siege took place in 587-86 B.C. and lasted a year and a half (see Jer. 52; 2 Kings 25).

About 70 years after this capture of Jerusalem in 605 Cyrus the Persian allowed the first contingent of Jews, led by Zerubbabel and Jeshua, to return to Palestine (see Ezra 1). It must be, then, that this is the beginning of the "seventy years" during which the Jews would "serve the king of Babylon" (Jer. 25:11-12). No other period quite fits the historical situation and Jeremiah's actual words.

2. The Providence of God

> And the Lord gave Jehoiakim king of Judah into his hand, with part of the vessels of the house of God ... (Dan. 1:2).

This gives a true interpretation of history. Just as there is "no restraint to the LORD to save by many or by few" (1 Sam. 14:6) so there is no restraint to destroy by many or by few. Later in the book (4:17) the rule of God in history is made even more plain.

3. The Transportation of Temple Vessels

> ... which he carried into the land of Shinar to the house of his god; and he brought the vessels into the treasure house of his god (Dan. 1:2).

This was to show the Jews that God would not protect even the holy vessels of His holy house from desecration by heathen hands if they, His people, would use them for unholy purposes. They were to learn, as American Christians need to know, that God is not a synonym for good fortune or prosperity, and that His places and emblems of worship are not mere good luck pieces. The rest of the vessels were carried away 20 years later (Jer. 52:17-23).

4. The Transportation of Daniel and His Friends

And the king spake unto Ashpenaz the master of his eunuchs, that he should bring certain of the children of Israel, even of the seed royal and of the nobles; youths in whom was no blemish, but well favoured, and skilful in all wisdom, and endued with knowledge, and understanding science, and such as had ability to stand in the king's palace, and that he should teach them the learning and the tongue of the Chaldeans (Dan. 1:3-4).

The office of Ashpenaz, "master of his eunuchs," is prophetically significant. Long before, in the days of Hezekiah, when he had inadvisedly admitted Babylonian diplomatic representatives to the temple, Isaiah had prophesied the loss of the temple vessels to Babylon (see 2 Kings 20:12-17). Then he ominously added in verse 18: "And of thy sons that shall issue from thee . . . shall they take away; and they shall be eunuchs in the palace of the king of Babylon." Eunuch (*saris*) in the Hebrew language designates a castrated or emasculated male. For obvious reasons eunuchs were frequently the officials in charge of royal harems. By a kind of metaphorical use of the word other officials were sometimes called eunuchs. There seems to be no reason in this case, aside from our natural revulsion at the idea, to suppose that Daniel and his friends did not submit to this mutilation. The sins of fathers are sometimes visited upon the children in divine providence.

Josephus quotes from Berosus, an ancient Greek historian, the following very interesting account of the circumstances and manner of Daniel's trip to Babylon.

When Nabolassar, father of Nabuchodonosor, heard that the governor whom he had set over Egypt . . . had revolted from him . . . committing certain parts of his army to his son Nabuchodonosor, who was then but young, he sent him against the rebel Nabuchodonosor, joined battle with him, and conquered him, and reduced the country under his dominion again. Now it so fell out, that his father Nabolassar fell into a distemper at this time, and died in the city of Babylon, after he had reigned 29 years. But as he understood, in a little time, that his father... was dead, he set the affairs of Egypt and the other countries in order, and committed the captives he had taken from the Jews, and Phoenicians, and Syrians... to some of his friends, that they might conduct that part of the forces that had on heavy armour, with the rest of his baggage, to Babylonia; while he went in haste, having but a few with him, over the desert to Babylon; whither, when he was come, he found the public affairs had been managed. ... Accordingly, he now entirely obtained all his father's dominions.

Daniel must have been in the group that took the long way home, northward to Euphrates, and thence southeastward along its banks to Babylon.

5. Training of Daniel and His Friends for Court Service

And the king appointed for them a daily portion of the king's dainties, and of the wine which he drank, and that they should be nourished three years; that at the end thereof they should stand before the king (Dan. 1:5).

These boys were taken from the "seed royal" and nobility in order to break the spirit of rebellion at Jerusalem. The particular ones chosen for the training were selected for their suitability to be trained for court service. The term "youths" is indefinite as to age. In view, however, of the training and growth designed for them as well as the fact that Daniel lived on for some 70 years, we may suppose they were in their "teens." "No blemish... well favoured" indicates they were to be good physical specimens and handsome. The wisdom in which they were to be trained was the technical and proverbial lore of the day—the cultural equivalent of science and philosophy today. "Knowledge" means "intelligence" here, and "science," "education." "Ability... to stand in the king's palace" designates the poise necessary for the public eye. They were the physical, intellectual, and moral cream of the crop, and being "seed royal," that is, of the king's kinfolk, of the best families, socially speaking. These were true advantages, not fully appreciated in our present democratic epoch, when "average" seems "normal," hence best.

"The learning and tongue of the Chaldeans" were possibly the ancient religious ritual and language of the Sumerians, earlier inhabitants of Babylonia, whose religion and culture had been taken over by the Assyrians and Babylonians.

All this was pagan education at its devilish best (or worst). Nothing could have been better designed to win them away from the faith of their fathers. It was, however, scarcely less geared to draw the young away than the modern secular education which prevails in colleges and universities today. Our cultural centers are still in the hands of the wicked one. Together with many false cultural values they purvey a philosophy which denies the existence of any God who can even "peep or mutter" (Isa. 8:19; 10:14), much less "bring every work into judgment" (Eccl. 12:14) or save a soul through faith in God's only begotten Son.

II. THE IDENTITY OF THE CHIEF ACTOR AND HIS ASSOCIATES (Dan. 1:6-7)

Now among these were of the children of Judah, Daniel, Hananiah, Mishael, and Azariah. And the prince of the eunuchs gave names unto them: unto Daniel he gave the name of Belteshazzar; and to Hananiah, of Shadrach; and to Mishael, of Meshach; and to Azariah, of Abed-nego (Dan. 1:6-7).

The changing of the names of the four youthful captives is most significant. It was designed to wean them from their old culture, language, and religion and join them to another—especially another religion. "Daniel" in Hebrew means God's prince (or judge). The new name, Belteshazzar (the same as that of the later king, Belshazzar) means Bel's prince. It honors one of the chief deities of Babylon (see Isa. 46:1; Jer. 50:2; 51:44). Hananiah means mercy of the Lord, being a variation of the Hebrew name, John. His new name, Shadrach, means the command of Aku (moon god). Mishael means, Who is like God? Whereas, Meshach means, Who is like Aku? Azariah means whom the Lord helps; Abed-nego, servant of Nebo. (Some recent findings modify these meanings.)

It is this group of four God-fearing youths who become the main actors in the crisis of right behavior immediately to follow and in the entire Book of Daniel.

III. EVENTS PLACING THE AUTHOR IN THE POSITION HE HOLDS THROUGHOUT THE BOOK (Dan. 1:5-20)

In addition to an explanation for the high position of Daniel and his three friends in the later history, this portion furnishes an outstanding example of spiritual and moral heroism.

Our own period, aptly dubbed "the ease era," does not have the climate which produces many heroes. The average American, including many who are already parents and a few grandparents, has yet to be involved in an unavoidable choice involving the necessary risk of his physical safety or public reputation. We prefer to *watch* synthetic heroes on television rather than even to *read* about authentic ones—much less *to be* real heroes!

Our era needs some heroes, too. We need them in public civic office no less than in the pulpit and mission stations; in newspaper offices as well as on the judge's bench, and in a professor's chair.

1. The Crisis of Right Living

> And the king appointed them a daily provision of the king's meat, and of the wine which he drank: so nourishing them three years, that at the end thereof they might stand before the king (Dan. 1:5).

Something about the wine and the meat (food) was defiling for these youths to partake. It is a naive supposition that some alcoholic content of the wine was the cause of defilement. There is no reason to believe that this wine was more alcoholic than the common wine the boys had drunk every day from infancy. The defilement was evidently connected with the fact that it was "the king's" food and drink. The word for defilement (v. 8) sometimes means physical defilement, as in Isaiah 63:3, where it is translated "stain" (as of garments). It sometimes means moral defilement, as at Zephaniah 3:1 where it is translated "polluted." It is more frequently to be understood as ceremonial (or religious) defilement (see Ezra 2:62, Neh. 7:64). In view of our Lord's familiar dictum that "not that which goeth into the mouth defileth a man" (Matt. 15:11) the possibility of moral defilement hardly seems possible. It must also be remembered that although the Old Testament furnishes many warnings by precept and example against the danger of drunkenness, complete abstinence is not commanded. Furthermore, since the food and drink were "the king's," it would not have been physically contaminated. The only likely possibility is therefore ceremonial defilement.

Among the ancients, religion was not a department of life to be cared for once a week, it was rather something that conditioned all of life, including eating and drinking. The preparation of food involved religious ritual and had mystic significance. Portions were offered to household deities. Slaughtering of animals among pagans, as well as among Jews, was a religious act to be carried out with proper solemnities. The flesh of animals from the king's table, and the wine as well, would first have been offered to the god of the king. To eat flesh sacrificed to a pagan god was forbidden (see Exod. 34:15), for it involved "serving other gods" in the public mind (see Hosea 9:3-4 and Ezek. 4:13-14).

A further problem was involved in the fact that Nebuchadnezzar's food would not have been prepared according to Levitical procedures, that is, it was not "kosher" (see Lev. 3:17; 6:26; 17:10-14; 19:26).

It is an indication of what God counts important that so many verses of a truly great book are devoted to discussing what four men did about a small religious scruple which had no evident practical importance. Sacred Scripture frequently devotes more space to religious minutiae than to the rise and fall of empires. It may seem to be a matter of slight importance whether one confesses Jesus to be *like* God or the *same as* God—yet the very integrity of our faith hangs on that distinction. It may seem like an unimportant hairsplitting distinction to insist that an objective propitiation of God's wrath (see Rom. 3:25; 5:9) was accomplished at Calvary rather than a *mere* demonstration of love, but again the very integrity of our salvation is at stake in the distinction. Furthermore, moral scruples may be quite as important as these theological ones. The fixing of a definite "back home" hour for one's adolescent son or daughter can be a distinctly necessary moral scruple which must be kept. Standards of "dating," counting money, places of entertainment—and a host of other things may take on high moral and spiritual importance. Especially where promises to parents, school rules, and so forth, are involved; these things become matters for resolute spiritual decision. It may come as a shock to learn that God once destroyed two young priests "on the spot" at the scene of their carelessness in observance of a seemingly unimportant matter of religious ceremony (see Lev. 10:1).

2. The Decision for Right Living

> But Daniel purposed in his heart that he would not defile himself with the portion of the king's meat, nor with the wine which he drank: therefore he requested of the prince of the eunuchs that he might not defile himself (Dan. 1:8).

In spite of all that has been said above about the ceremonial defilement involved in eating Nebuchadnezzar's food, the fact remains that in extreme cases, when necessary to sustain life, the Jews were conscience-free to violate these things (see Matt. 12:3-5; 1 Sam. 21:6; Num. 28:8-9). Daniel refused, however, because he saw the intent of the king was that, through these things, he could wean Daniel from his faith. Calvin well says, Daniel "simply determined in his heart not to taste the diet of the court, desiring by his very food perpetually to recall the remembrance of his country. He wished so to live in Chaldea, as to consider himself an exile and a captive, sprung from the sacred family of Abraham."

Had Daniel been one of the easygoing Christians of our day who is prepared to let any worldly pleasure or entertainment, earthly gain or excitement, be an excuse for setting aside the claims of the Lord upon him, we would never have heard of this firm choice of his. But then, we would never have heard of Daniel either! He certainly would never have adopted "safety first" as his slogan! What worldly people call squeamishness may be truly a matter of principle.

3. Procedures for Right Living—the Elements of Moral Heroism (Dan. 1:8-14)

It is in these seven verses that the heart of the story of Daniel's moral heroism lies. In order better to understand the fine points of the narrative, and as a step preliminary to pointing out, in order, the precise elements of this heroism, we will examine closely some of the language.

> ... therefore he requested of the prince of the eunuchs that he might not defile himself (Dan. 1:8).

The Hebrew language is replete with words which might be translated "requested." This one is usually translated "seek." It never appears except in what is called an *intensive* stem. The word cannot be used to describe any mild or indifferent entreaty. An idea of the nature of the entreaty here is indicated by the fact that the word is used of David's importunate prayer to God for the life of his first child by Bath-sheba (2 Sam. 12:16).

> Now God had brought Daniel into favour and tender love with the prince of the eunuchs. And the prince of the eunuchs said unto Daniel, I fear my lord the king, who hath appointed your meat and your drink: for why should he see your faces worse liking than the children which are of your sort? Then shall ye make me endanger my head to the king (Dan. 1:9-10).

God provides defenders for His own in strange places and from unexpected sources. This also shows that admirable motives and sentiments are not absent from heathen hearts. They not infrequently put some Christians to shame by their genuine concern for the needs of other people. It was, for example, a harlot of Jericho who sheltered the spies sent to that city by Joshua: the reason was that God had touched her heart. Wherever it appears, love is a "fruit of the Spirit." The rule is that "the tender mercies of the wicked are cruel" (Prov. 12:10).

What Daniel specifically asked is not stated. At this stage, whatever the specific request may have been, it evidently was neither granted nor denied. The prince of the eunuch's answer simply made it discourteous for Daniel to pursue it further.

> Then said Daniel to Melzar whom the prince of the eunuchs had set over Daniel, Hananiah, Mishael, and Azariah, prove thy servants, I beseech thee, ten days; and let them give us pulse to eat, and water to drink. Then let our countenances be looked upon before thee, and the countenance of the children that eat of the portion of the king's meat: and as thou seest, deal with thy servants (Dan. 1:11-13).

Observe that the author, guided by the Holy Spirit's own point of view, does not deign to recognize the new names honoring the pagan gods of Babylon. He uses their proper Hebrew names.

"Melzar," it is now generally agreed by scholars, means "the steward," a name for the man's office, not for the man.

"Pulse" probably should read "vegetables." The objections to the king's food were based on the ground that, containing slain flesh improperly prepared, it was ceremonially unclean. This was not the case with vegetables.

"As thou seest, deal..." probably means no more than that Daniel was prepared to accept it as the will of God for them to ignore the ceremonial impurity of the king's food if God did not miraculously (or providentially) intervene. As stated above, if necessary to sustain life, or if God specially commanded, "unclean" food could be eaten (see above on v. 8 and also Ezek. 4).

Daniel's proposition appealed to the steward as sensible and feasible. What the results would have been if they had not fared well on the diet is not stated. Likely neither the steward nor Daniel and his three friends knew exactly. He, as well as they, wanted the plan to succeed—they were crossing their bridges as they came to them. The situation called for no ordinary amount of diplomatic dexterity on the part of all concerned.

For the instruction and enlightenment of a hundred generations, this story presents the elements present in true Christian heroism. If we want heroes to emulate, here are some of them. We shall see good reasons why Daniel is called a man "greatly beloved" (9:23; 10: 11, 19) and why Ezekiel's prophecy links him in character with Noah and Job (see Ezek. 14:14, 20).

A. Discernment. Daniel and his friends saw what was evil in the diet prescribed by the king's officials. The specific items of diet were likely the same as they had been eating all their lives, and hence, the defilement involved was not obvious. The risk of defilement, however, was recognized.

Where did Daniel learn such discernment? We do not know just how much schooling Jewish boys of those days had, but we do know the Mosaic commands about parental training of children (see Deut. 6:4-9). The credit, then, must go to Daniel's parents. The application to present-day situations is obvious.

One wonders what happened to the multitudes of other Jewish boys transplanted into a pagan culture. Evidently most of them went the way of Babylon.

We live in a time when most boys are being taken away from their home and church surroundings into the worldly and frequently defiling atmosphere of military training or of university education. Our girls likewise too often go out unguarded and unprepared to meet the temptations of study on the university campus or at work and play in the pagan city. If our young people are to retain their purity, they will need to have a basis for spiritual discernment brought from home.

B. Resistance to evil. There was steel in this young man's character. Separation from home, distance from family observation, and relative immunity from criticism did not make him a pushover for the tempter.

Again, where did Daniel get this fiber? This inner strength of soul? The answer is the same as before—from parental training. Children are by nature undisciplined. There is nothing, in fact, quite so against the nature of the young as to resist temptation where food and drink are concerned. The numerous "cookie jar" jokes are a bit of evidence of this. Yet children must be taught to resist the desire to eat all the time, and to eat anything that appeals to the natural appetite. For the sake of health, as well as for the sake of spiritual welfare, they must learn to resist temptation. For a very few children precept and example may be enough—perhaps Samuel was this kind of child. But nearly all children need to experience some kind of pain, inflicted by the hand of the parent, when the rules are broken. Parents who wish to rear sons and daughters who will resist evil when away from home will so manage their homes that they must, on pain of punishment, resist temptation at home (see Heb. 12:9-13; Prov. 3:11-12, 13:24; and 1 Sam. 2:12-36, note v. 29).

C. Power to say no! He purposed in his heart that he would not defile himself—and he said so! He declared himself. By doing so he not only put himself on record but the force of his example carried others with him and won the respect of unbelievers. This force of character does not ordinarily develop in youth. Youth is a season of conformity. At the height of the Second World War a few college girls (in the absence of men from the war-time campuses) started wearing men's wool shirts, tails dragging at their calves, across the campus walks. In a few weeks thousands of men's shirts had been sold to college girls. Some of the young ladies looked like nothing quite so much as bags stuffed with watermelons—but they wore the shirts just the same. Why? No power to say no to a ridiculous fad. Such matters are quite harmless. But there are other areas—the wearing of immodest apparel, for example (see 1 Peter 3:1-5; 1 Tim. 2:9)—where the possibility of harm in conformity is great. We do not need nonconformity for the sake of difference; what we need is nonconformity for Jesus' sake (see Acts 4:19-20).

D. Physical courage. If the prince of the eunuchs felt that he would endanger his head if he granted Daniel's request, then Daniel likewise would endanger his head to persist in his request. The man who threatened his own college of wise men with slaughter and the reduction of their houses to dunghills (Dan. 2:5) for failure to do the manifestly impossible was not one to be trifled with.

It is sad that the customary picture of the Christian missionary, even of our Lord Himself, in the popular mind, is that of a bloodless weakling. Quite to the contrary, the roster of the spiritual giants is a list of courageous men. Luther risked his life at Worms, Calvin at Geneva, Savonarola at Florence, Huss at Constance, Paul at Jerusalem. Within recent decades in New Guinea and in Ecuador stalwart young men have lost their lives for Jesus' sake—and there have been many others.

Daniel had no way of knowing that his brave action would lead to political power at a later time. He sided with truth and right when they were unpopular.

E. Perseverance. Daniel did not accomplish his purpose to change the food order "in one jump" so he took another jump. The story relates that after he failed with the prince of the eunuchs he tried with the steward. The bare request had failed, so next time he joined a workable and sensible proposition with the request. The same ingenuity at finding loopholes in the law, for which youth is famous, was here directed toward plugging all the holes!

F. Determination. "Daniel purposed in his heart." He knew what his goals were and he determined to attain them.

Daniel got his goals from the Holy Scripture and from pious training in godliness. We will gain good goals and determination to follow them from the same sources. Christ is the Christian's goal for living. In the words of Paul: "To live is Christ, and to die is gain" (Phil. 1:21).

G. Meekness. There is not the slightest evidence of mock heroics, bravado, or of disrepect for authority in Daniel's behavior. Daniel did not loudly stand on any alleged "constitutional rights." Rather he "requested" or "besought" the prince of the eunuchs. And to the steward Daniel humbly said, "I beseech thee." Such meekness is always a sign of greatness. There is none greater in the Old Testament story than Moses. Yet of him it is written, "Now the man Moses was very meek, above all the men which were upon the face of the earth" (Num. 12:3).

H. Wisdom, or good sense. Not only his discreet manner of approach to his masters, but also in his sensible proposal—a 10-day trial—is this demonstrated. Already in his own lifetime his wisdom was proverbial as the expression, "wiser than Daniel" (Ezek. 28:3) shows.

4. The Rewards of Right Living (Dan. 1:15-21)

In the first place, the four boys fared better physically (v. 15). This was not due to the superiority of their diet, but to the overruling providence of God. It was at this point in the story that God is first seen to assert His power over the Babylonians.

In the second place, their right living, or perhaps it might better be said, their right choosing, was rewarded by deliverance from any necessity for ceremonial defilement. They had honored God, so God honored them. They had trusted in the Lord with all their hearts; they had not leaned on human understanding. They had acknowledged Him in all their ways. As a result God had directed their paths (see Prov. 3:5-6).

In the third place, all four of the "children" gained increased knowledge and skill, especially Daniel who gained understanding of visions and dreams—used with good effect later. Verily, "to him that hath shall be given." The "fear of the Lord is the beginning of wisdom."

In the fourth place, they gained preeminence among all their associates. Again, it is written: "Seest thou a man diligent in his business? he shall stand before kings; he shall not stand before mean men" (Prov. 22:29, Dan. 8:27).

Finally, Daniel was granted a continuing influence in high places for a period of about 70 years, even on into the period of the Medes and Persians who replaced the Babylonians in rulership of the Near East. "And Daniel continued even unto the first year of king Cyrus" (v. 21). This was at least till 539 B.C., and perhaps even as much as 15 years longer, that is, at least for a period of 66 years after Daniel's transportation from Jerusalem. No Hebrew mentioned in the Old Testament, outside of Joseph in Egypt, ever had influence in the affairs of nations like that of this man Daniel.

Conclusion

This chapter has set the stage for understanding the rest of the Book of Daniel. In doing so it has imparted a lesson in moral heroism. This chapter also demonstrates how God's Word, the Bible, gives emphasis to the truly important things. One verse only is devoted to the fall of Jerusalem and another to the professional education of the four boys, but almost half a chapter is devoted to detailed recital of the story of what might appear to be a trifling religious scruple. What takes place in a young child's heart, or in a midweek evening prayer meeting in a small church may be more important to God than what happens in the capitals of the world. Further, observe how God, as usual, operated through a minority—a remnant, if you will. Thank God for his faithful minority!

Daniel 2

Nebuchadnezzar's Dream of a Great Image:

A Prophecy of the "Times of the Gentiles"

I. The Reception of the Dream (Dan. 2:1)

II. The Test by Use of the Dream (Dan. 2:2-6)

III. The Revelation of the Dream (Dan. 2:7-23)

IV. The Telling of the Dream. (Dan. 2:24-35)

V. The Interpretation of the Dream (Dan. 2:36-45)

VI. The Rewards for Interpretation of the Dream
 (Dan. 2:46-49)

For all who take the Bible seriously as an interpreter of the past and present as well as a dependable guide for the future, this is one of its most important chapters. In addition to being one of the longest chapters in Scripture, it is unique in giving the first schematic presentation of how God is ordering the course of the ages toward their final consummation in Christ. He who is working "all things after the counsel of his own will" (Eph. 1:11) has not let history slip out of His all-embracing grasp. Rather, Scripture refers to God's providential control as His "dispensation [management] of the fulness of times [that is, the full course of all history]" that "he might gather together in one all things in Christ" (Eph. 1:10).

Many twentieth century thinkers have come to have a new appreciation of the Bible as being the true original source of the idea that history does have a goal, that it is "going somewhere." The pagan notion of antiquity (reflected in the "under-the-sun" philosophy of Ecclesiastes, see 1:1-11) was that all events of history run in cycles of repetition. Like the seasons, which repeat themselves every year, reasoned the philosophers, what is happening now has happened in the past, and will continue to repeat itself.

While the chapter before us gives no specific information concerning particular nations now in existence, it does supply much information concerning specific tendencies now in evidence and operation. For this reason no one is really equipped to give a biblically informed Christian interpretation of current history apart from this chapter, for some of it appears nowhere else in Scripture.

At first glance, it may seem a bit strange that the prophetical dream herein should first have been granted to a heathen monarch, for ordinarily God reveals His secrets to prophets (see Num. 12:6). A bit of reflection will recall at least three previous scriptural instances wherein heathen potentates received prophetic revelations (see Gen. 20:3-7; 2 Chron. 35:20-22).

Our procedure for study of this long, difficult, and in places somewhat obscure, chapter will be as follows. We will give careful attention to understanding the narrative and its divine interpretation. After this study, we will seek to apply it to personal life and the current world scene.

I. THE RECEPTION OF THE DREAM
(Dan. 2:1)

And in the second year of the reign of Nebuchadnezzar, Nebuchadnezzar dreamed dreams; and his spirit was troubled, and his sleep went from him (Dan. 2:1).

The terrifying effect of the dream upon the king is hard to explain if, as is suggested by first impressions from the Authorized Version, the king had forgotten what was in his dream. He might have had a kind of emotional "hangover" from a forgotten nightmare; but nothing, it seems, as terrifying as this to a hard-bitten character like the mighty Nebuchadnezzar, general of armies and master of men. As will be seen shortly, perhaps the king was frightened precisely because he had *not* forgotten his dream.

II. THE TEST BY USE OF THE DREAM
(Dan. 2:2-6)

A minor problem of interpretation, unrelated to the message of Daniel occurs in this portion in connection with the sentence: "Then spake the Chaldeans to the king in Syriack" (v. 4). This does not mean that the language in which the Chaldeans spoke was Syriack. Rather, as is now generally recognized by scholars, "in Syriack" (Heb., in Aramiac) should be regarded as an ancient editorial rubric indicating that all that follows in Daniel, down to the end of chapter 7 is in that language.

As just observed, the Authorized Version gives the reader the impression that the king could not recall the dream and that he asked the wise men to recall the dream because he had forgotten it. The portion in question is the expression in verse 5: "The thing has gone from me," repeated in verse 8. The margin of the American Standard Version gives this reading: "The king answered and said to the Chaldeans, The word is gone from me: if ye make not known unto me the dream and the interpretation thereof, ye shall be cut in pieces...." This sense is employed in the Revised Standard Version also. The essential change is that "thing" is rendered "word" in the sense of decree or commandment. The king, if this be correct, had not forgotten the dream at all; but rather, since he did remember the dream, was using it as a test of the reliability of the wise men's alleged occult powers. They who could produce supernatural interpretations, unknown except to themselves and the gods, ought to be able to produce the dream known to the king. The dream, common to mortal man, ought to be more easily produced, the king seems to have reasoned, than the interpretation, available only from the gods. The king, on this view of the matter, was simply reasoning from the greater to the less.

This offers the correct sense, and for the following reasons.

(1) The word *millah* (Aramaic) employed here is commonly given either translation—word or thing. Thus there is a wide-open possibility that the translation should be "word." It is, indeed, the more common translation. This very term, *millah,* appears also in modern Israeli Hebrew where it is used in the name for a dictionary, that is, a book of words.

(2) Right in the immediate context (v. 9) the word *millah* is translated "word," "... ye have prepared lying and corrupt words." It is clear, on this account, that Nebuchadnezzar was familiar with this use of the word and was thinking of it in that sense at the time.

(3) If the king had not forgotten his dream, we have a plausible explanation as to why the wise men did not at least try to invent a dream and interpretation by giving the king a whole-cloth fabrication of some sort. Any kind of story would have been worth a try since their lives were at stake.

(4) It likewise gives a fuller meaning to verse 9. Nebuchadnezzar felt that the wise men were withholding information that they might give if they wanted to do it—or at least might be withholding information. To him it appeared they might

only be waiting "till the time be changed," that is, till the position of the stars in the zodiac would change so it would be impossible to secure the astrological data necessary.

The occult advisors (wise men) are of interest as showing upon whom the ancient world of men, without knowledge of the God of truth, relied for guidance into the unknown future. Verse 2 mentions 4 classes of them. *Magicians.* The Aramaic *chăr-tŭm-mîm* means scribes, or those learned in books, perhaps incantors. Religious formulas likely were in the Sumerian language of the predecessors of the Babylonians, unknown to ordinary citizens. Incantations were in this long-dead foreign tongue. *Astrologers* (*ashapîm*). A better translation is practicers of hidden arts—like the present day "spiritualists." They were not "star-gazers" as "astrologers" suggests. *Sorcerers* (*mekash-shepîm*). Derived from a word meaning to cut, the name refers to their work of cutting into small pieces the ingredients of various magical drugs and potions, as in Chinese pharmacy. *Chaldeans* (*kasdîm*). In this case the name refers to a class of wise men, though Chaldeans may be a comprehensive name for all the wise men (see vv. 4 and 10).

These men were the scholars of the ancient world. They were for that age what the scientists of our research laboratories and the university professors are to our age. The perspective of history labels them fools. Will the perspective of the future say the same of our modern wise men? Without indicting research or education, as such, of any inherent error it can safely be said that in the present era our "post-Christian" scholars quite commonly share four essential defects with those of pagan antiquity.

There is *first* a common essentially pantheistic view of nature. Such deity as is held to exist is locked up in the system of nature. He is not nature's creator, nor its Lord; rather only some vital principle within nature. In the *second* place there is common to both an essentially optimistic view of man. Man, himself, is not the root of human disorder but the problem is his environment or his "fate." *Third*, both operate in essential ignorance of God's ordering of history by a wise and all-powerful providence. Neither knows of history's goal wherein God will sum up all in a consummation. *Fourth*, both operate in the absence of any permanent system of values. The glory of the God and Father of our Lord and Saviour Jesus Christ, the only true measure of ultimate worth, is almost wholly unknown and unconsidered.

III. THE REVELATION OF THE DREAM
(Dan. 2:7-23)

1. The Failure of the Wise Men (Dan. 2:7-12)

They answered again and said, Let the king tell his servants the dream, and we will shew the interpretation of it (v. 7).

No doubt the wise men were sincere enough in claiming that the king's refusal to comply with their request was unfair (v. 10). They had their professional procedures. Their formulas were standardized, and evidently all of them applied to the interpretation of dreams rather than to the recovering or discovering of them.

... There is not a man upon the earth that can shew the king's matter: therefore there is no king, lord, nor ruler, that asketh such things at any magician, or astrologer, or Chaldean. And it is a rare thing that the king requireth, and there is none other that can shew it before the king, except the gods, whose dwelling is not with flesh (vv. 10-11).

Observe that the wise men at least believed in the possibility of divine revelation of the future as well as divine revelations of the unknown past. The Bible claims, in the Genesis account of the creation, to contain an account of things God revealed to Moses concerning the manner in which the universe originated. No man was there to observe it. It was to be forever unknown to man unless God chose to reveal it. The Bible likewise claims to have predicted details of the coming of the Saviour long before His birth—as well as the 70 years of servitude of the Jews to Babylon and many other things. It claims also to give us important details concerning our own personal future in a heaven or hell, concerning future resurrections, judgments, and final rewards. The Holy Scriptures purport to outline certain future events in the course of the world's future history. So these ancient "quacks" were nearer to biblical truth than are some preachers and theology professors of our day. To reject predictive prophecy out of hand is to reject the authority of the Bible.

That Nebuchadnezzar's rage was excessive and that his pronouncement was harsh is readily granted. But that his anger was unjustified and some pronouncement of punishment wholly unjust may not be granted. His excesses need not be defended, but that the king's judgment was essentially in error cannot be granted. These men professed to know the divine mind. They claimed their positions and support from this alleged knowledge. The king's test was valid. If they were failures they were also frauds. "The thing has much deeper and farther-reaching implications. It furnishes demonstration of the imcompetence of all mere human resources, learning, and power to ascertain the mind and will of God apart from His own revelations" (Joseph Seiss).

2. The Success of Daniel (Dan. 2:13-23)

The same discretion that had won the master of the eunuchs and the steward (see 1:2-16) now prevailed with the captain of the king's guard (2:14-15). Just how Daniel conveyed to the king his request for time is not stated. Probably some messenger carried the message.

The Lord alone could save these Hebrews and Daniel knew it. But just like the rest of us, even a Daniel could exercise a stronger brand of faith in the company of others likeminded, so he laid the matter before his three companions (v. 17).

It is significant that their prayer was frankly (even frantically) selfish—"that Daniel and his fellows should not perish with the rest of the wise men of Babylon" (v. 18). Even the Son of God prayed for Himself (see Matt. 26:39, 42, 44; John 17:5). We are encouraged to pray for ourselves—our needs, our ailments, even our desires, if they are not wrong desires (Psa. 21:2; 38:9). Later in the book, Daniel is presented as a great intercessor.

God's answer came "in a night vision" (v. 19). Nebuchadnezzar had first received the matter in a dream. The vision, an experience of seeing things brought before the mind's eye, might be a part of a dream (cf. 7:1) but not invariably so.

Daniel's prayer of thanksgiving, verses 20-23, is a truly beautiful poem or psalm in the spirit and fashion of the biblical Psalter. His prayer recognizes God's control over the history of nations, which is significant in connection with the interpretation of the vision. It praises God for His wisdom and thanks Him for granting the same wisdom to Daniel.

IV. THE TELLING OF THE DREAM
(Dan. 2:24-35)

The first report of success was to Arioch (v. 24). Though introduced simply as "captain of the king's guard" (v. 14), the sinister nature of his work is emphasized in some of the translations—"captain of the cutthroats," Spanish; "chief butcher," Greek of Septuagint and of Theodotion. Even so he was not untouched by Daniel's appeal. It is not difficult to understand why Daniel let no grass grow under his feet in reporting his success at discovery of the king's dream.

This Arioch is of some interest as likely a typical "bureaucrat" of the day. It had been at his recommendation that delay had been granted in the first place, and since he had thereby risked the king's disfavor, he too reported to the king "in haste" (v. 25). Now, as the time-serving opportunist that he was, he claims credit for search and discovery of the new master of dreams. He declares: "I have found a man ... that will make known unto the king the interpretation" (v. 25).

Against this background of the perversity of the "natural man" (1 Cor. 2:14), the moral glory of Christ in the heart and action of Daniel the "spiritual" and "wise" man (see Mal. 3:16-18; 1 Cor. 2:15), is in stark contrast. Daniel now gives God all the glory (vv. 27-28)—as indeed he should. If there is any realm wherein God alone can enter without help, it is knowledge of the future.

The most important part of this section is the statement in verse 28 and 29 of the *scope* of the predictions in the interpretation to follow. These two verses provide the key to the predictions of chapter 2, which, in turn, furnishes the framework of all the prophecies of the rest of the Book of Daniel. Daniel, in turn, is the key to the chronological framework of the predictions of the rest of biblical prophecy. Hence, it is hard to exaggerate the importance of these two verses.

> But there is a God in heaven that revealeth secrets, and maketh known to the king Nebuchadnezzar what shall be in the latter days. Thy dream, and the visions of thy head upon thy bed, are these; as for thee, O king, thy thoughts came into thy mind upon thy bed, what should come to pass hereafter: and he that revealeth secrets maketh known to thee what shall come to pass (Dan. 2:28-29).

The scope of the predictions of "what shall come to pass" is indicated by two expressions: "in the latter days" (v. 28) and "hereafter" (v. 29). Concerning the former, "the latter days," we must strongly emphasize that we must not focus the reference to events of the consummation at Christ's second advent. It is a phrase out of the general prophetical literature of the Old Testament wherein it refers to the general future, in contrast to "the former days." This phrase especially refers to the future as it develops and is concluded in the messianic period of the world's duration. See Isaiah 2:2; Micah 4:1; Genesis 49:1 especially in context, and Jeremiah 48:47 for proof of this point. The "last days" include both first and second advents of Christ, as well as the period between them in which we now live. All the Church Age is a part of these "last days." An examination, in context, of the following passages will satisfy the inquiring student on this point—Acts 2:17; cf. Joel 2:28; 1 John 2:18; Hebrews 1:1-2. Thus, while the prophecy does relate to times of consummation at the end of this age, it also covers the interval intervening.

"Hereafter" has no direct reference to human existence after death as in popular parlance. In this context it refers simply to the succession of kingdoms to follow Nebuchadnezzar's, reaching down to the coming of Christ. The two advents of Messiah are not clearly distinguished in this or in any other Old Testament prophecy, both being blended in one great complex of events. Progress of history and of revelation since Old Testament times distinguishes the two advents.

The great metallic image needs no elaboration. One's own body will furnish a sketch on small scale of what the king saw on a grand, gigantic scale. It was in such magnificent splendor that even to a king like Nebuchadnezzar, accustomed to glitter and show, it appeared bright and excellent, for "the form thereof was terrible" (v. 31). Neither is there anything essentially obscure about the stone and the action of it. These all call for special attention in connection with the interpretation now to follow.

V. THE INTERPRETATION OF THE DREAM
(Dan. 2:36-45)

1. The Head of Gold

> Thou, O king, art a king of kings: for the God of heaven hath given thee a kingdom, power, and strength, and glory. And wheresoever the children of men dwell, the beasts of the field and the fowls of the heaven hath he given into thine hand, and hath made thee ruler over them all. Thou art this head of gold (Dan. 2:37-38).

It represents Nebuchadnezzar himself, and as seen later, also his kingdom and dynasty. Other Old Testament prophets had used gold as a symbol of Babylon (see Isa. 14:4). It is to be noted that this grant from God included the whole earth. Though Nebuchadnezzar never got around to possessing all of it, his empire did probably reach much farther than the area of the fertile crescent to which it is customarily assigned. Our information is not complete by any means, but it is now known that he defeated the Pharaoh of Egypt and conquered

Syria, Palestine, and Phoenicia. Phoenician colonies ringed the Mediterranean. He may, therefore, have received revenues from the entire Mediterranean world.

2. The Breasts and Arms of Silver

> And after thee shall arise another kindgom inferior to thee ... (Dan. 2:39).

This must be compared with the corresponding description of the image (v. 32). History and the Bible both agree that the kingdom which succeeded Babylon was that of Medo-Persia. The last chapter of 2 Chronicles is very clear on the point. Furthermore, Daniel himself, a bit later, says: "Darius the Median took the kingdom" (5:31, cf. 5:28). Yet when the law of that kingdom was promulgated it was the "law of the Medes and Persians" (6:8). The duality is suggested by the two arms and two breasts.

3. The Belly and Thighs (Aramaic, buttocks) of Brass

> ... and another third kingdom of brass, which shall rule over all the earth (Dan. 2:39).

Again historians and the Bible are in agreement. This is the Grecian nation led by the Macedonian kingdom of Philip and his son, Alexander the Great. The Old Testament story ends before the coming of the Greeks as conquerors into the Near East. That it was the Greeks who were to succeed the Medes and Persians is made crystal clear by Daniel in his eighth chapter (vv. 20-21). Joel 3:6 also mentions the Greeks. Alexander led his armies into Asia Minor from Macedonia in 334 B.C. Then in a series of engagements over the following three years he became master of the Medo-Persian Empire.

4. The Legs of Iron and Feet of Iron and Clay (Dan. 2:40-43)

Rome and the great civil, legal, and religious system which accompanied Rome are represented by this part of the image. This cannot be proved by citing references in the Bible which say that Rome succeeded to the empire of the Greeks, for there are no such texts. Rome probably did not yet exist in the sixth century B.C. At least no extensive kingdom of that name existed. There is, however, sufficient evidence that the Rome which history knows as following the last stage of the Grecian period is at least included in the fourth empire seen in this prophecy. This evidence is due to the fact that the fourth empire, which had no existence yet in Daniel's time, is given most detailed treatment in the prophecy. This is a divine providence.

This is, we repeat, a prophecy of Rome, its empire, and the world system it introduced and which, it seems, is to prevail until Jesus comes again. The details fit. Rome was "strong as iron"—of all common metals the strongest. "It breaketh in pieces" aptly describes the effect of Roman policy on all other nations and their institutions. It "subdueth all things" also fits Rome. Edward Gibbon wrote: "The empire of the Romans filled the world, and when the empire fell into the hands of a single person the world became a dreary prison for his enemies. To resist was fatal, and it was impossible to fly" (*Decline and Fall of the Roman Empire*). The two legs may symbolize the twofold division which came between the eastern and western portions in the imperial period, with capitals at Constantinople and Rome.

There is a real and important sense in which all the "West," or European civilization, is a continuation of the old Roman world. It is likewise true that, thus applied, it continues to "subdue" and "break in pieces" all (that is, all other nations, cf. v. 40). Constantinople, the eastern capital of the empire, held out against all attackers until it fell to the Turks in 1453. The "Holy Roman Empire" continued in name in the western part of the empire until abolished in 1806 by Napoleon. The "West," however, continues to be Roman. Our literature (including grammar itself) as well as much of our law, and even our popular religion are borrowed from Rome. Christendom itself became Romanized whether Eastern (Greek-speaking) or Western (Latin-speaking). This Western form of things continues to subdue the world, to break apart social customs and institutions and then reform them according to Western patterns. It is a Western form of Christianity that has planted our faith around the world in the last two centuries. The very language of the New Testament was the language of Rome—not Latin as might be supposed, but Greek.

In verses 42-44 the "toes of the feet" are picked out for special interpretation. In the opinion of many interpreters, they represent a final form of Gentile dominion under 10 allied kings in the times of the Antichrist. They are probably the same as the final Gentile kings of earth as seen in Daniel 7:24 and Revelation 17:12.

A question frequently asked is: Does this mean there will be a revival of the Roman Empire? The answer depends somewhat on whether "revival" be understood as resurrection of a dead thing or not. If it does, then the answer is in the negative. The fourth kingdom of the prophecy endures until the establishment of the kingdom of Christ on earth (as symbolized by the stone). That the headquarters of the empire shall be reestablished at Rome is doubtful, though certainly possible.

Before presenting the final elements of the prophecy some general principles about the course of world dominion through the centuries as seen herein must be observed. Four principles are seen to prevail.

A. A continuous succession of world dominions down to the coming of Messiah's kingdom. As observed earlier, the prophecy covers the "latter days," inclusive of all time from Daniel's own down to the consummation. There is not the slightest hint of or basis for introducing a "gap" or "hiatus" somewhere. Jesus refers to this sweep of Gentile rule when Jewish political power is gone as "the times of the Gentiles" (Luke 21:24). At the end of it Jerusalem is to cease to be "trodden down" by Gentiles and will again be the seat of national sovereign government. We should not, therefore, expect some other shape of Gentile sovereignty before Jesus comes again.

B. A progressive division of sovereignty, reaching a climax in the 10-toed stage of the image prophecy. An illustration will help. Monarchy is rule by one; obligarchy, rule by a few; democracy, rule by all citizens. Sovereignty (that is, right of rule) is progressively divided in the illustration. So in the image that right of rule is in the head, the absolute monarchy of Nebuchadnezzar. But it is progressively divided till at the end it is divided between 10 (toes) representing 10 kings ("the days of these kings" of v. 44) of Daniel 7:7. This may refer to the present divided state of the Roman dominion, but it seems more likely to refer to some situation at the end (cf. Rev. 12:3; 13:1; 17:3, 7, 12).

C. A progressive deterioration in the character of the authority of rulers. This decline is indicated by four elements in the dream. There is, first, a deterioration in the *worth* of the metals: gold, silver, copper, iron (and clay). The second is in *position* in the image from gold on top through silver and brass to iron at the bottom. The third is the prophetic interpretation of verse 39: "... after thee shall arise another kingdom *inferior* to thee." Finally, observe that the metals grow *lighter* in weight (this is, in specific gravity, mass per unit of volume), from the heaviest in gold to the lightest in iron and clay.

See how this deterioration has worked out in history. Nebuchadnezzar (gold) had what James the Second of England only thought he had—divine right monarchial power. Jeremiah 27:5-8 and Daniel 5:18-19 make this plain: "Whom he would he slew and whom he would he kept alive." The Medo-Persian kings who followed Babylon were not above the law as Nebuchadnezzar was, but were subject to the laws of the realm—bound by the legal entanglements of their own decrees (see Dan. 6:14-15). The Greek kings had no dynastic claims in the East at all, but ruled solely by virtue of great personal gifts. The Roman emperors, and even the early kings of the dynastic period, before republic and empire, ruled largely by popular choice. Republicanism, which followed the monarchial period, soon degenerated into mob rule especially after it merged with the Imperial period. Some of the greatest emperors were affected by the will of mobs in the capital city. Since those days, with a checkered history of changes and variety during the Middle Ages, democracy has emerged—that is, sovereignty has been shared with everyone.

D. A progressive improvement in hardness and strength. An exception is the clay, which, though hard enough in a vitrified form to cut iron, is very brittle. This indicates, perhaps that the kingdoms will grow stronger. At the end the brittleness of mass sovereignty is indicated by the clay. That the people in general are signified is a quite natural interpretation supported by general usage even today in aphoristic speech. The races were created of "dust of the ground" (Gen. 2:7); the Hebrew word for mankind, *adhamah,* means ground; more than once in Scripture the "people" are spoken of metaphorically as "the clay" (Isa. 45:9, 64:8, cf. Rom. 9:21).

5. The Stone Which Smites the Image and Becomes a Great Mountain

And in the days of these kings shall the God of heaven set up a kingdom, which shall never be destroyed: and the kingdom shall not be left to other people, but it shall break in pieces and consume all these kingdoms, and it shall stand for ever. Forasmuch as thou sawest that the stone was cut out of the mountain without hands, and that it brake in pieces the iron, the brass, the clay, the silver, and the gold; the great God hath made known to the king what shall come to pass hereafter: and the dream is certain, and the interpretation thereof sure (Dan. 2:44-45).

Here is unquestionably represented the coming of the Messiah and His kingdom, just as the head of the image stood for Nebuchadnezzar and his kingdom. No symbol of Scripture speaks more uniformly and pointedly of the Saviour than does the stone. Genesis 49:24 is the first appearance of the thought: "... from thence is the shepherd, the stone of Israel"—combining the stone symbol with the figure of the shepherd (Ps. 23; John 10; 1 Peter 5:1). At Psalm 118:22 the

Saviour, as the rejected stone later to be exalted to chief cornerstone, is first introduced. This is followed by another form of the figure, oft cited by New Testament writers, as in Isaiah 28:16 where our Lord is said to be Zion's foundation stone, tried and true, one on whom the believing soul may find a sure foundation.

To the *nation of Israel* Christ was and remains "the stone of stumbling, and for a rock of offence . . . for a gin and for a snare to the inhabitants of Jerusalem" so that many of them should "stumble, and fall and be broken, and be snared, and be taken" (Isa. 8:14-15). It is known from the New Testament, as indeed, the centuries since likewise show, that this has been fulfilled. As Paul says, Jesus was "to the Jews a stumblingblock" (1 Cor. 1:23). Peter declares that He is to Jews "a stone of stumbling and a rock of offence, even to them which stumble at the word, being disobedient" (1 Peter 2:8). The tragic results were prophesied by Jesus (see Luke 19:41-44).

To *Christian believers* Christ, quite to the contrary, has always been a sure foundation stone, "to whom coming, as unto a living stone, disallowed indeed of men, but chosen of God, and precious . . . a chief corner stone" (1 Peter 2:4-7). Indeed He has been such a stone to believers of all ages (see 1 Cor. 10:4; cf. also Deut. 32:4, 15, 18, 30-31, 37).

Unhappily, but necessarily, Christ the Rock has another relationship—to the *unsaved nations* of the world—that of a smiting, smashing, grinding stone. Jesus once said that the kingdom of God would be taken from the Jews and given to Gentile believers. Because of their unbelief the Jews were judged and of that judgment Jesus said: "Whosoever shall fall on this stone shall be broken: but on whomsoever it shall fall, it will grind him to powder" (Matt. 21:44). This is precisely what is going to happen one of these days when Jesus comes again—no more as suffering servant and tender shepherd but as judge (see Matt. 25; Rev. 19:11). It is precisely in this capacity and relationship that the coming of Christ "in his kingdom" is prophesied here.

But, someone wants to know, is it not the first coming of Christ which is predicted here? Those who expect a peaceful epoch on earth to be followed by the Second Coming of Christ (Postmillennialism) feel that the "smiting stone" predicts the first coming of Jesus and that the kingdom of the stone is the Church. Those who expect neither a future visible reign of Christ on earth, nor a millennium of peace before Jesus' second coming (Amillennialism) agree. Those who interpret the twentieth chapter of Revelation mainly literally believe that whatever fulfillment the symbolism of the stone may have in the first advent, the main reference is to the second advent. Some arguments in favor of this view, known as Premillennialism, are as follows.

A. By other views the church, which has no civil prerogatives at all (unless the traditional Roman Catholic theory is right), appears to be made into a political entity like Babylon, Medo-Persia, and so forth. On the contrary the church, both as a body and individually, is to be "subject to the powers that be" (Rom. 13:1) and is to "render" obedience dutifully "unto Caesar" (Matt. 22:21).

B. Contrary views substitute a quiet imperceptible growth of a church in a gradual conquest for what the passage presents as a violent, catastrophic, sudden blow upon the consummate form of Gentile dominion.

C. The violence with which Christ's kingdom is presented as replacing the kingdoms of this world fits expectation of a day when "he shall smite the earth with the rod of his mouth, and with the breath of his lips shall he slay the wicked" (Isa. 11:4). Compare also Zechariah 14:16-19. In this connection it is written of God's Son: "thou shalt break them with a rod of iron; thou shalt dash them in pieces like a potter's vessel" (Ps. 2:9). Note also Revelation 19:15: "And out of his mouth goeth a sharp sword, that with it he should smite the nations: and he shall rule them with a rod of iron." Another text states: "for the nations and kingdom that will not serve thee shall perish: yea, those nations shall be utterly wasted" (Isa. 60:12).

D. The church has not overcome the kingdoms of the world, and if we interpret the Scriptures correctly, it never will. It seems that those who, like Amillenarians, expect no future reign of Christ on earth, and who expect good and evil to grow together till the harvest at the end of this age (see Matt. 13:30, 39-40) are inconsistent in identifying this victorious "stone" kingdom with the church. The Postmillenarians appear to be unbiblical in the expectations of a victory of the church over the world. (See also 2 Tim. 3:1-5 and 1 Tim. 4:1-3.)

The kingdom of Christ, symbolized by the stone that becomes a great mountain and fills the whole earth, is of great importance for Christians. Perhaps we can explain it somewhat like this: Our Lord did establish a kingdom when He first came—a realm in which He now rules in believing Christian hearts. It is a kingdom of "righteousness, and peace, and joy in the Holy Ghost" (Rom. 14:17). It is a present kingdom of God's "dear Son" into which believers have already been translated (Col. 1:13), and where we are now reigning with Him. His reign in heaven was inaugurated at His session at the Father's right hand (Acts, chap. 2). But there is another aspect of this kingdom still wholly future, when "the kingdoms of this world . . . become the kingdoms of our Lord, and of his Christ; and he shall reign for ever and ever" (Rev. 11:15). For this kingdom we can only pray, as taught, "Thy kingdom come, Thy will be done in earth as it is in heaven."

VI. THE REWARDS FOR INTERPRETATION OF THE DREAM (Dan. 2:46-49)

It is a matter of encouragement to all sorely tried believers to note that the faithful prayers and testimony of Daniel brought about a change in the heart of the proud and arrogant king. It wasn't conversion, and he had many lessons yet to learn (see chap. 4). Nevertheless, he did come to see that Daniel was indeed a true servant of God and that his God was "God of gods, and Lord of kings, and a revealer of secrets" (v. 47). This was at least progress.

Further, this act of Daniel brought him into a position of favor among unbelievers, a circumstance which made it possible for him to serve God better, and to help men more. That his Jewish brethren in exile knew about him and regarded him well is evidenced by the high praise given him by his contemporary and companion in exile, Ezekiel (see Ezek. 14:14, 20; 28:3).

Some of the greatest of comforting truths in all the Bible are found in the chapter we have now surveyed. Foremost of these is the fact of divine providence—the overruling control which He has over all. He works everything "after the counsel of his own will" (Eph. 1:11). This being true, we know that this world is not ultimately going to go to smash. Over all from the fall of rain drops to the fall of empires, God rules and reigns. Because this is true the saint of God can know that "all things work together for good to them that love God" (Rom. 8:28). This is—not because of fate or some impersonal optimistic destiny—but because the God who rules is the believers' Father.

Another impression remains with the discerning and impressionable reader—that no matter how pretentious and impressive any government or capital may seem to be, it is not permanent and the judgment of God has been pronounced upon it. Our own nations of today, with whatever affection we hold them, are not exceptions. Hitler built his *Reich* to last, he thought, for 1,000 years. It lasted less than 10. Every new alliance, each new precarious balance of power, is formed to ensure a "just and lasting peace." These efforts are praiseworthy. We should pray for the blessing of God on the worried men who try to work them out (see 1 Tim. 2:1-3). But we dare not put our trust in men. Our ultimate hope is in the living God rather than in men of this world, for the present age is destined for judgment.

Finally, we should be warned in our study not to rush off too quickly in search of "practical" lessons in preference to factual, historical, doctrinal matters. Nothing is ultimately more practical than a correct understanding of the words of Jesus about His kingdom. The key, however, to those words lies right here in these chapters, for on them Jesus built His own teaching about the kingdom of God. The pearls of God's treasure will not be found by the callow, shallow, or the slothful scholar. Nor will the impatient reader understand the "mysteries of the kingdom."

3

Daniel 3

Three Heroes in a Fiery Furnace:

A Lesson in Steadfast Faith

I. The Opposition to Faith (Dan. 3:1, 8)

II. The Temptation of Faith (Dan. 3:2-15)

III. The Demonstration of Faith (Dan. 3:16-18)

IV. The Salvation Wrought through Faith (Dan. 3:19-20)

This chapter of the Bible contains one of the most famous stories in the world. In other days and in other lands than ours, where physical peril from the wrath of wicked men has been far more real, this story has encouraged many. Assurance has come to God's oppressed people of the truth that "the fear of man bringeth a snare: but whoso putteth his trust in the Lord shall be safe" (Prov. 29:25). The story's fame extends even to the well-known recital of historical examples of faith in the eleventh chapter of Hebrews. After listing some of those "who through faith subdued kingdoms, wrought righteousness, obtained promises, stopped the mouths of lions," mention is made of those who through faith "quenched the violence of fire" (Heb. 11:34). The three young Jews of this chapter must surely be the heroes of faith.

There are no clear predictions in chapter 3. It consists simply of a narrative of the trial of faith imposed upon three believing young men by their ungrateful professional associates. The "cast of characters" is already familiar. Nebuchadnezzar has figured prominently in the two previous chapters. The "Chaldeans" (v. 8) are the same "quacks" who failed their king as advisors and interpreters in the text connected with the kings's dream. The pious Jewish boys had previously honored their God, and this they did by refusing to defile themselves with the king's food and drink. Furthermore, to the obvious chagrin and envy of the Chaldeans, they had just now been promoted to high administrative positions in government of the home province of Babylon.

The absence of Daniel has set off what is probably the oldest manhunt in history—a quite tame one, of course, in the commentaries. Was he unable to be present on account of illness? In later life he was sometimes ill for days and absent from the places of the king's business (see 8:27). Did his high office as president of all the "learned societies" (2:48) excuse him from the necessity of being present on the occasion of the dedication of the image? This is doubtful. Or, was he simply "out of town on business" for the king? This has a kind of ludicrous sound, but it may be nearest the truth.

I. THE OPPOSITION TO FAITH (Dan. 3:1, 8)

Nebuchadnezzar the king made an image of gold, whose height was threescore cubits, and the breadth thereof six cubits: he set it up in the plain of Dura, in the province of Babylon (Dan. 3:1).

The image itself, its size, shape, composition, and significance draws first attention. The height of 60 cubits (about 90 ft.) would have made it visible for a distance of 12 to 15 miles in all directions on the broad lower Mesopotamian plain. The height suggests, since it was only nine feet thick, that most of the monument was a pedestal.

The language, "an image of gold," requires only that it should have been covered with gold. In Old Testament times it was customary to overlay religious objects of non-precious material with a covering of gold (cf. Isa. 40:19, 41:7; Jer. 10:3). The word for image used here is *tselem* common to several Semitic languages, meaning primarily shadow or, by extension, a material reproduction of the outline of some living thing. The ordinary meaning would be statue; but sometimes this word *tselem* can describe a pillar, obelisk, or stele only partially sculptured with a relief. So this may have been a pillar with either a statue or relief at the top. The ancient world was fond of gigantic statuary.

Though there are reported to have been three places in Mesopotamia called "Dura" in ancient times, only one is near the city of Babylon. At this site (Tells of Dura) there are reported to be ruins which may even be related to this image and its platform.

The question of to whom or to what the image was dedicated is of greater importance for interpretation of the passage, but impossible to decide with complete certainty. The fact that several times worship of the image is distinguished from worship of the gods of Babylon indicates that it was not dedicated to any particular Babylonian deity (v. 14—"do not ye serve my gods, nor worship the golden image which I have set up?" also vv. 12, 18). Several scholars argue that it was a symbol of Nebuchadnezzar's empire. This is plausible, especially in connection with the dream of chapter 2. This would account for the fact that representative officials from all sections of the empire were required to be present and why when the three Jews refused to render to the image the required worship, the Chaldeans could charge Shadrach, Meshach, and Abed-nego with treason rather than sacrilege (v. 12). Furthermore, just as the "head of gold" in the image stood for Nebuchadnezzar and his empire, so the statue may have been dedicated both to the empire and its king. Another most attractive suggestion is that Nebuchadnezzar had been so impressed by Daniel's revelations from Jehovah, the Jewish God, that he had the image erected and dedicated in honor of the God of Israel. Far-fetched as this may seem, it is by no means impossible. The image would thus take somewhat the same status as the altar "to the unknown god" of the Areopagus (Acts 17). Furthermore it is not without precedents. Aaron's golden calf (Exod. 32) and Rehoboam's two calves of gold (1 Kings 12:25-33), both used for idolatrous worship, were certainly dedicated to Jehovah. It is precisely this perverted kind of worship which was Israel's most acute temptation—worship of the true God in an utterly false manner. This continues today in different ways to be a great temptation.

> Wherefore at that time certain Chaldeans came near, and accused the Jews (Dan. 3:8).

The significance of these words is chiefly that they show how the chief opposition to the obedient faith of God's people often comes from other people. The men, in this case, were the very professional class of wise men, advisors of the king, to which our three heroes belonged. They were professional associates, in a sense.

Either good or evil men may oppose us, that is, tempt us to be less than God's will prescribes for our lives, but the temptation most frequently comes, as in this story, from those who do not love God. Our three heroes did not fear them. "The fear of man" only "bringeth a snare" (Prov.

29:25). The worst, Jesus has said, that evil men can do to us is to harm our bodies. Since God, however, can destroy both the soul and the body in hell we should "fear" Him. So, "beware of men," Christ says (Matt. 10:17), not because they themselves can really harm you ultimately but because they can lead you to sin. Yet, further on, Jesus says, "fear them not" (Matt. 10:28), inasmuch as their power to do harm extends only to our bodies.

II. THE TEMPTATION OF FAITH (Dan. 3:2-15)

Perhaps before proceeding it will be well to answer a question: What is temptation? In the Bible the word "temptation" is simply an alternate term for test or trial. In this broad sense, illness, poverty, and so forth, are temptations. In this sense of trial even God is tempted (see Exod. 17:2, 7; Deut. 6:16). In the special sense in which we now usually think of it, however, temptation is a test in the moral or spiritual realm. It consists of enticement to sin. It may be external stimulation of improper desires, as in the case of the serpent's tempting Eve (see Gen. 3:1; cf. 1 Tim. 2:14), or of David's temptation by sight of a particularly alluring woman (2 Sam. 11:1-4). Or, it may be something that arises from within man's nature without the necessity of external stimulation, such as pride, gluttony, covetousness, and so on.

There is a sense in which it is true that God never tempts any man. James says: "Let no man say when he is tempted, I am tempted of God, for God cannot be tempted with evil, neither tempteth he any man: but every man is tempted, when he is drawn away of his own lust, and enticed" (James 1:13-14). Yet in an indirect manner, called providence, God does try men. "The righteous God trieth the hearts and reins" (Ps. 7:9, cf. Job. 7:18; Psa. 11:4-5; 139:23). God also allows Satan to be an instrument of trial.

> Then an herald cried aloud, To you it is commanded, O people, nations, languages, that at what time ye hear the sound of the cornet, flute, harp, sackbut, psaltery, dulcimer, and all kinds of musick, ye fall down and worship the golden image that Nebu-

chadnezzar the king hath set up: and whoso falleth not down and worshippeth shall the same hour be cast into the midst of a burning fiery furnace (Dan. 3:4-6).

This proclamation presented a threefold temptation to the three Jews—as well as to the many others to their nation who may have been present.

It was first of all:

1. Temptation to Perversion of Their Faith. Idolatry in Israel as noted above had been always mainly a perversion of the true worship of the one true God rather than a denial or abandonment of it. The gods of their neighbors were worshiped occasionally, to be sure. But the idolatry of Israel was usually an attempt to worship Jehovah-God through some "aid to worship" such as a graven or molten image. This was clearly true of the first case after the Exodus, the golden calf incident in the wilderness, for when Aaron announced: "These be thy gods, O Israel, which brought thee up out of the land of Egypt" (Exod. 32:4), he used the plural name *Elohim,* the word usually translated simply, God. So the plural *Elohim* should be understood in the sense of God instead of gods. Moreover, the whole affair was preparation for what Aaron further declared would be "a feast to the LORD" on the morrow (Exod. 32:5). The next day Moses came down from the mountain only to find the people engaged in drunken, licentious, pagan-style dancing around a golden image of a calf—all in the name of Jehovah.

We may rightly discern in the worship of idols a perversion of a normal and healthy desire in man for a visible manifestation of the Godhead. That is, it is not entirely wrong to prefer to walk "by sight." Philip quite guilelessly suggested: "Shew us the Father, and it sufficeth us" (John 14:8). As Jesus then pointed out to Philip, it is precisely to satisfy this longing of men that God, in part at least, sent His Son to be "God manifest in the flesh." "The Word [Christ] became flesh" John says, "and lived for a while among us" (John 1:14 NIV). The Christian may, then, find a fully sufficient answer to this longing to see the living God by reading the scriptural account of the life of Jesus.

2. Temptation to Compromise Their Faith, that is, to worship an idol and to justify it somehow as a means to some good end.

A second look at the three confessors is in order. They were three of the very finest physical and intellectual specimens their nation could boast. They had been chosen for training in the highest learning their age knew. They had achieved the very highest kind of success their profession offered. Moreover, they had been advanced to honors most unusual. These honors had all come to them as foreigners and—what is far more important—it had all happened to them while they were very young men.

These three urbane and cultured, yet godly, Jews quite naturally wanted the approval of their professional associates in Babylon. By joining in worship of the idol they might have had it. They might have agreed among themselves that the idol was nothing and that they should join in the external acts of obeisance to keep up appearances while inwardly reserving all worship for Jehovah. Or, they might have joined in the idolatry and have excused it to themselves as something they were compelled to do.

Yet, they steadfastly refused to worship the hateful idol, choosing what was, humanly speaking, certain death, rather than to pervert in any manner their pure faith in the invisible God. It was this God who had commanded: "Thou shalt not make thee any graven image, or any likeness of any thing that is in heaven above . . . thou shalt not bow down thyself unto them, nor serve them: for I the LORD thy God am a jealous God . . ." (Deut. 5:8-9). This God had also said, "Thou shalt have none other gods before me" (Deut. 5:7). One thinks also of James' words: "Ye adulterers and adulteresses, know ye not that the friendship of the world is enmity with God? Whosoever therefore will be a friend of the world is the enemy of God" (James 4:4).

3. Temptation to Concealment of Their Faith.

> Nebuchadnezzar spake and said unto them, is it true, O Shadrach, Meshach, and Abed-nego, do ye not serve my gods, nor worship the golden image which I have set up? (Dan. 3:14).

The text above should be changed to read "Is it on purpose?" instead of "Is it true?" The situation seems to have been that the king was genuinely fond of the three young men who had previously served him very well. So, after having been informed that they had not joined in worship of the image, the king, though exasperated with a disobedience he could not understand, still wished to spare them if possible. So he suggested that perhaps the failure to join in the worship had not been "on purpose." If they would only say the failure was unintended, then they would live. A little white lie would have saved them.

> Now if ye be ready that at what time ye hear the sound of the cornet, flute, harp, sackbut, psaltery, and dulcimer, and all kinds of musick, ye fall down and worship the image which I have made; well: but if ye worship not, ye shall be cast the same hour into the midst of a burning fiery furnace; and who is that God that shall deliver you out of my hands? (Dan. 3:15).

This verse indicates that the temptation was made almost irresistibly appealing. Having been brought to the very jaws of death by their initial steadfastness, the very goodness of the king in offering them a second chance—a chance that appears to have involved the entire repetition of the ceremonies for their special benefit—must have strongly impelled the confessors to abandon their intransigent position.

This is the fourth and last enumeration of the musical instruments used in the Babylonian "orchestra." Six different instruments, as well as "all kinds of music" are mentioned.

This verse directs an important truth our way: that God's name and reputation are intimately connected with the obedient faith of His people. Nebuchadnezzar had learned to browbeat his own gods. If they would not help him, he could stop supporting their temples and feeding their priests. So he was quite prepared to declare that the Jewish God of Shadrach, Meshach and Abed-nego was not one that "shall deliver you out of my hand." In spite of the admirable earlier confession of chapter 2 (see v. 47), Nebuchadnezzar had not yet learned well enough that the Jewish people not only were different on account of their faith, but that their God was different.

III. THE DEMONSTRATION OF FAITH (Dan. 3:16-18)

> Shadrach, Meshach, and Abed-nego, answered and said to the king, O Nebuchadnezzar, we are not careful to answer thee in this matter (Dan. 3:16).

There has been some discussion as to whether or not the manner of address involved disrespect for the king, and if their answer displayed arrogance. Some say that they were both disrespectful and arrogant. We think not. It is better to say that now the final impasse had come there was no need for further palaver. If they had explained their real reasons for defying the king's order he would not have understood anyway. After all, there really is no courteous way to say some things. When they said, in effect, "There is nothing more to say," it is true.

> If it be so, our God whom we serve is able to deliver us from the burning fiery furnace, and he will deliver us out of thy hand, O king (Dan. 3:17).

It is hard to find any lack of confidence in God's ability to save them. The opening words, "If it be so" appear to express a kind of sublime, but very practical, lack of further concern about mere talk. Perhaps these troublesome words mean, "Even if there might be some use for further talk as far as you are concerned, our words are at an end." It should be noted they had received no revelation as to whether or not God would preserve them alive through the furnace. God, as they knew, is quite chary in use of miracles. There was no obvious reason why Jehovah should make a special case of these Jews' extremity and perform a miracle to save them. God often lets his faithful martyrs (martyr means "witness") die for their faith. So, when they said, "he will deliver us out of thy hand, O king" they may have been quite grimly conscious of several possible ways in which deliverance from the king might take place. It might be by death. Death puts a blessed end to persecution from man. It delivers the Christian into the tender hands of God and transports him into the bosom of Abraham. So, whatever the fire might do they were: "Safe in the arms of Jesus, Safe on His gentle breast."

Deliverance might also come by a miracle. But they knew it was by no means certain, for they had no promise of it.

> But if not, be it known unto thee, O king, that we will not serve thy gods, nor worship the golden image which thou hast set up (Dan. 3:18).

The expression of doubt implicit in "But if not" does not imply any doubt as to God's power, but rather of what has been called "ethical ability." That is, they were by no means sure what the good providence of God would make necessary. If God had good reasons for letting some "martyr blood" tell the world about Himself they would die. If His plans could be better served, say the encouragement of other persecuted Jews, by being delivered alive—then they would be delivered alive.

There are at least four elements common to all overcoming Christian faith demonstrated in these verses. Their faith, in the first place, was a *full committal.* "We are not careful to answer thee" (v. 16), or "There is no need for further talk." This was the only answer Nebuchadnezzar received to his question, "Was it on purpose?" This cast the die. From here on there was no turning back. How important it is that faith be a final act never to be reversed or repented of! In the second place their faith involved *full confidence* (v. 17). "Our God whom we serve is able," they declared. They understood, as all should, that to deny God's omnipotence is really to deny His existence. This was their answer to the king's blatant question: "Who is that God that shall deliver you out of my hands?" (v. 15). In the third place, there is a *reckless-ness of faith* to be observed. Verse 18 fairly rings with this quality. They answered the implied question of the king, "What are you going to do?" In faith they declared: "We will not!" This element of recklessness, however, would have been quite foolish if it had not been for still another element, foundational to all the others: *full knowledge.* They *knew* that God would deliver in one way or another because they *knew* their Hebrew Scriptures. The mighty works of God at the time of the Exodus and at other junctures in their history as well as their own recent experiences in connection with the king's dream simply left no room for doubt in their pious hearts. It is this which accounts not only for their commitment, confidence, and recklessness but for these qualities of faith in all ages. Any believer can join in so claiming: "So that we may boldly say, the Lord is my helper, and I will not fear what man shall do unto me" (Heb. 13:6).

IV. THE SALVATION WROUGHT THROUGH FAITH (Dan. 3:19-20)

Then was Nebuchadnezzar full of fury, and the form of his visage was changed against Shadrach, Meshach, and Abed-nego: therefore he spake, and commanded that they should heat the furnace one seven times more than it was wont to be heated. And he commanded the most mighty men that were in his army to bind Shadrach, Meshach, and Abed-nego, and to cast them into the burning fiery furnace (Dan. 3:19-20).

There was immediate abandonment of any tentative plans for a repetition of the ceremonies. Their seeming contemptuous refusal even to recognize benevolent intentions on the king's part angered him beyond measure. The Aramaic words used are all of the utmost force in expressing anger. The furnace was to be heated seven times hotter than customarily. ("One seven" is merely literal rendition of Aramaic idiom. The word "one" may be omitted in translation.) The mightiest, that is, the leading generals and military men, were to execute the sentence. A description of the furnace is not given here. But in the manner of ancient smelting furnaces, it was probably a kind of silo constructed of brick and built into a mound or hillside with draft openings at the lower end at ground level and with flue opening at the top. Presumably entrance for the victims of this manner of execution was made at the top through which the flames and smoke were belching. The king commanded the furnace to be heated seven times hotter than usual. This should be understood, like "ten times better" (1:20), as an extreme superlative rather than in any exact sense. We speak the same way outside of circumstances where exact measurements are necessarily understood, as in a laboratory or weather bureau.

Curiosity asks for some information as to the fuel for the fire. It is not known, except that the usual fuel in those days would have been charcoal. Dr. R. Payne Smith suggests that oil and naphtha were added. Presumably by naphtha he means petroleum. (Naphtha is originally the Assyrian or Babylonian word for petroleum.) Petroleum and natural asphalt have long been used in that part of the world.

> Then these men were bound in their coats, their hosen, and their hats, and their other garments, and were cast into the midst of the burning fiery furnace (Dan. 3:21).

The significance of this verse is in the fact that immediately and unceremoniously these men were thrown to the fire in the very clothes they wore. Ordinarily men wear special clothes for an execution and any articles of finery would be removed (for example, the crucifixion of Christ), but on this occasion the king was in a big hurry. Strangely enough, no translators or commentators ancient or modern have attained any degree of certainty as to the meaning of the names rendered here "coats," "hosen," and "hats." When the Septuagint (Greek) translation was made, about two centuries before Christ, the names had already been forgotten; for that version shows ignorance on the part of the translators. This in itself is a very strong argument for the sixth century genuine origin of the book, for a man writing in the very era in which the Septuagint arose would have used currently understood words which the translators also would have understood. Their outer garments, especially their turbans, were apparently stripped off and used as cords to bind them.

> Therefore because the king's commandment was urgent, and the furnace exceeding hot, the flame of the fire slew those men that took up Shadrach, Meshach, and Abed-nego (Dan. 3:22).

These verses remind us how Nebuchadnezzar was in reality an *absolute* monarch. Precautions could have been taken which would have enabled the executioners to cast the three confessors into the fire without causing any loss of life besides. But, on account of the king's unreasoning mad fury, they were not taken. This king, as the Bible bears some record, and as secular history and archaeology also bear out, was capable of acts of true greatness. He was interested in architecture, art, literature, and even archaeology. He was known to be affectionate and kindly with his family. But in a rage he was a veritable devil, careless of the lives and feelings of even his most loyal subjects.

It was their religion, that is, the doctrines of it and the appropriation of them, that had made these fearless Jews what they were. Their Scriptures told them that there is one true God, that they were personal beings as He is, and made in His likeness. They further knew that He is an ethical being (that is, righteous) who expects His people to be the same; that He is not, like the many gods of the heathen, a petulant lord to be patronized, but an all-powerful, all-knowing, all-holy person to be obeyed. In such a climate of belief the conscience grows in strength, it is guided by right knowledge, it issues in the virtues of love, mercy, fairness—and above all—of loyalty and trustworthiness.

> Then Nebuchadnezzar the king was astonied, and rose up in haste, and spake, and said unto his counsellors, Did not we cast three men bound into the midst of the fire? They answered and said unto the king, True, O king. He answered and said, Lo, I see four men loose, walking in the midst of the fire, and they have no

hurt; and the form of the fourth is like the Son of God (Dan. 3:24-25).

These words must be interpreted in the light of the king's own level of understanding. He was not trained in the Scriptures, hence, knew nothing of the second person of the Trinity whom Christians know to be our Lord Jesus Christ. A fair translation of his declaration would be, "the form of the fourth is similar to a son of a god." His declaration is similar to that of that other pagan, the centurion who superintended the execution of Jesus, and who exclaimed from the depths of his pagan heart, "Truly this was a son of a god." We cannot make either of these confessions mean anything like the great confession of Peter: "Thou art the Christ, the Son of the living God" (Matt. 16:16), or that of Thomas, "My Lord and my God!" (John 20:28).

The faith of these men had won a fivefold victory.

(1) By faith they were loosed from their bonds (v. 25). This was literally true, for the king saw the man "loose." Morally speaking, there is also a great freedom of soul when one makes that final plunge of commitment to God, expecting nothing from man, knowing all things are his in God.

(2) By faith they were protected from all harm (v. 27). The fire could not harm them. They were not even touched by the smell of smoke. Only those who work around wood fires can have the "poetic" appreciation this deserves. Did you ever smell an Indian? If you say yes, you are mistaken. What you really smelled were his wood-smoked, buckskin moccasins. There is nothing quite like that odor—not unpleasant, but certainly unforgettable.

(3) By faith they were comforted in trial (vv. 24-25, 28). "One like a son of a god," as Nebuchadnezzar described him, is apparently none other than the great Angel of the Lord, the pre-incarnate Christ whom the New Testament identifies as the Son of God, our Lord Jesus. We are reminded of how the Lord stood by Paul (see Acts 25:10-11) in a similar situation, and of how on another occasion the Lord told him to be of good courage.

(4) By faith God was glorified (v. 29). This is, in certain respects, the high point of the chapter. Men realize the purpose for which they were made only when their lives give God glory. Even the heathen king was convinced. Brave Christian testimony will always produce respect for the witness of his God. Time-serving bowing and scraping never draw forth such admiration from kings for their underlings. These actions produce (and deserve) only disgust.

(5) By faith God's servants were rewarded (v. 30). The devout will remember "Be thou faithful unto death, and I will give thee a crown of life" (Rev. 2:10).

4

Daniel 4

The Dream of a High Tree:

A Lesson in Humility

I. Introductory Matters (Dan. 4:1-9)

II. Narration of the Dream (Dan. 4:10-18)

III. Interpretation of the Dream (Dan. 4:19-27)

IV. Fulfillment of the Dream (Dan. 4:28-33)

V. Conclusion: Restoration of the King (Dan. 4:34-37)

In the chapter before us is related the story of a heathen king in whom God took a great personal interest. It is true that He dealt with the king in judgment, but accompanying the judgment was a divine revelation which gave the king the meaning of the punishment, thus directing him toward moral improvement. That is, the punishment was gracious and corrective rather than penal. The fifth chapter of Daniel tells the story of another king (Belshazzar) to whom God sent judgment with an accompanying revelation—but in his case the judgment was wholly penal. It brought to an eternal end all hope for correction or improvement of the men concerned. In Nebuchadnezzar's case we are to regard the corrective judgments with accompanying explanations as manifestations of the "goodness of God" which according to Paul "leadeth thee to repentance" (Rom. 2:4).

Nebuchadnezzar's last words in the chapter that lies before us are: "Those that walk in pride he is able to abase." It is best to make one's self humble—before God has to make one so. How good it is, then, to heed the words, "Humble yourselves in the sight of the Lord, and he shall lift you up" (James 4:10).

I. INTRODUCTORY MATTERS (Dan. 4:1-9)

1. Salutation of a State Paper (Dan. 4:1-3)

> Nebuchadnezzar the king, unto all people, nations, and languages, that dwell in all the earth; peace be multiplied unto you (Dan. 4:1).

These words form the official address of what was originally a state paper of the second king of the Neo-Babylonian Empire, Nebuchadnezzar son of Nabopolassar. Although these words are in the Bible by the prophetic authority of Daniel, it seems clear that Daniel did not write them. Nebuchadnezzar speaks in the first person throughout, making indirect claim to authorship of it. The formal structure of the chapter, addressed to all the subjects of the king, shows it to be a public document.

Nebuchadnezzar left behind him many building inscriptions, inscribed memorial stones, and the like, in Mesopotamia and Syria. Those, now discovered and translated, run into hundreds of lines of translation. They show that the king took a personal interest in these writings, apparently composing many of them himself. Merodach, patron god of Babylon, is addressed and praised in most of them. As in our chapter, he frequently refers to himself in the first person and expresses himself in poetic parallels, as, for example, in verse 3 of the chapter before us:

> How great are his signs!
> and how mighty are his wonders!
> his kingdom is an everlasting kingdom,
> and his dominion is from generation to generation.

Among the many ancient writings of Nebuchadnezzar which recently have been recovered there has appeared no copy of this chapter of Daniel. No one should be surprised if it should happen, however. Stranger things have happened. The striking similarity of style, outlook, and ideas of Nebuchadnezzar's writings to the chapter before us strongly support the authenticity of our chapter.

> I thought it good to shew the signs and wonders that the high God hath wrought toward me (Dan. 4:2).

The miraculous events of Scripture are called "signs" because they have meaning or significance; "wonders" because they produce wonderment as effect among those who witness them.

The better rendering of "most high God," shows that Nebuchadnezzar, though evidently still a polytheist (cf. vv. 8-9), recognized the superiority of Jehovah the God of Daniel. The whole intellectual, moral and religious atmosphere of the ancient world made belief of a strict monotheistic sort difficult even for the Jews. Evidence is that the Jews only gradually came to believe in the nonexistence of their neighbors' gods and image worship. But, if even a wise and well-informed king like Solomon could lapse into idol worship, then we may be certain that belief in a plurality of gods had a firm grip on men's minds in ancient times.

This chapter, according to verse 2, is intended as Nebuchadnezzar's personal testimony of faith. It has an utterly sincere ring, like Peter's, "We cannot but speak the things which we have seen and heard" (Acts 4:20).

> How great are his signs! and how mighty are his wonders! his kingdom is an everlasting kingdom, and his dominion is from generation to generation (Dan. 4:3).

The exclamation of praise to God for His mighty works is the proper reaction of man to the attributes of God in manifestation, that is, God's deeds. The Bible presents such spontaneous expressions of praise as this of verse 3 as reaction to God's omniscience (Rom. 11:33); to His work of creation (Ps. 8:9); or to His benevolence (Ps. 107:8).

2. Circumstances at Court Leading Up to the Proclamation (Dan. 4:4-9)

The first circumstance was *successful accomplishment*. The king was "at rest" in his palace. This was the quiet that came as a result of his wars of conquest and completion of great construction projects in Babylon. It is the bright background against which the gloomy dream stands in contrast.

The second circumstance was personal and national *growth*. He was "flourishing in my palace." Ordinarily used of growing plants, the first readers would have thought of a luxuriant green vine in connection with "flourishing" (cf. v. 11). Thus the recital anticipates both the correspondence between the dream and the king's actual career and the contrast between the happy estate of the king before his insanity and humiliating degradation.

The next suggestion was *trouble* within. The king was prosperous and successful, but a frightful dream upset him. "Uneasy rests the head that wears the crown." The enemies outside the gates had all been subdued. But the natural man within the king himself was a dreadful enemy soon to break forth—"he that ruleth his spirit [is better] than he that taketh a city" (Prov. 16:32).

To add to the king's distress was *frustration.* Again he caused his wise men to be brought before him, and again they failed him (v. 7). Even though the task was simpler than that of producing both a dream and its interpretation as in chapter 2—they failed. It would seem from our point of view that this school of quack doctors should have been dismissed long since. They were failures (chap. 2) and they were jealous opponents of the ones who had discredited them (chap. 3). But evidently there was enough national and personal pride about the king that he would not dismiss these most prestigious representatives of the traditional heathen wisdom of his country.

There was finally an *appeal*—to the very man whom the king's pride had tried to ignore, Daniel the prophet. And since the interpretation Daniel gave of the king's former dream had not been hopeful for the indefinite continuation of Nebuchadnezzar's dynasty, he probably was more than a little afraid of what this frightening dream might portend in Daniel's view. Observe that the text does not say the wise men *could not* interpret the dream, but that they "did not" make it known. Actually the dream rather suggests a sad future even apart from special interpretation. It was a sad story to start with. Perhaps the wise men simply didn't have the courage to tell the king what they thought the dream portended. Daniel, the king could be sure, would always speak the truth.

II. NARRATION OF THE DREAM (Dan. 4:10-18)

1. The Tree

Thus were the visions of mine head in my bed; I saw, and behold, a tree in the midst of the earth, and the height thereof was great. The tree grew, and was strong, and the height thereof reached unto heaven, and the sight thereof to the end of all the earth: the leaves thereof were fair, and the fruit thereof much, and in it was meat for all: the beasts of the field had shadow under it, and fowls of the heaven dwelt in the boughs thereof, and all flesh was fed of it (Dan. 4:10-12).

Trees are the most useful of all plants. They provide fruit for man's table and food for beasts as well. They make shade and shelter for man and beast. Trees, therefore, are frequent biblical symbols. So it was no new symbolic motif that appears as a tree in the fabric of the king's dream.

The fact that the tree was seen "to the end of all the earth" suggests that the fame of the kingdom of Nebuchadnezzar was worldwide. The fact that beasts gathered beneath it and birds in its branches, and that "all flesh was fed of it" brings to mind that Babylon became a very great metropolis. Nebuchadnezzar and his successors are reputed to have stored immense quantities of grain and other foods within the city to care for the city's needs for many—some say 20—years.

2. The Watcher

> And I saw in the visions of my head upon my bed, and, behold, a watcher and an holy one came down from heaven (Dan. 4:13).

"Watcher" means "wakeful one" and is almost certainly a name for an angel. The ancient Greek version renders it "angel." The idea is of the wakefulness of those on guard. As watchers of God they are His "eyes." The word "and" between "a watcher" and "an holy one" means "even." That is, the watcher is a holy watcher. Note that the watcher, *even an holy one* is the singular subject of the next verse.

3. The Decree

> He cried aloud, and said thus, Hew down the tree, and cut off his branches, shake off his leaves, and scatter his fruit: let the beasts get away from under it, and fowls from his branches: nevertheless leave the stump of his roots in the earth, even with a band of iron and brass, in the tender grass of the field; and let it be wet with the dew of heaven, and let his portion be with the beasts in the grass of the earth: let his heart be changed from man's, and let a beast's heart be given unto him; and let seven times pass over him (Dan. 4:14-16).

These ominous details are the features of the dream, no

doubt, which had made the king afraid. They indicate the near destruction of the person in whose career the events are to take place. That it was a prophecy of a man rather than of a tree, as such, is indicated by the words of verse 16. The changing of the heart from a man to that of a beast could be predicated only of a man. These suggestions of unhappy changes in the future were sufficient to upset the "rest" of the king "flourishing" in his palace.

4. The Authority and Intent of the Decree

> This matter is by the decree of the watchers, and the demand by the word of the holy ones: to the intent that the living may know that the most High ruleth in the kingdom of men, and giveth it to whomsoever he will, and setteth up over it the basest of men (Dan. 4:17).

This verse is the very heart of the message of the Book of Daniel, and especially of this chapter. Couched in simple language as an explanation of the authority and intent of the decree of the angels concerning the dream it gives us the very key to the understanding of the affairs of men and nations of every age.

Observe in the first place that the angels of God, called watchers and holy ones, are the ones who speak here with God's authority. The ministry of angels in general and in relation to the giving of Holy Scripture in particular, is one of the most neglected areas of Bible study today. Yet, according to Hebrews 2:2, the entire Mosaic Law was mediated through angels. These angels appear often in the stories of the patriarchs. And, further on in this Book of Daniel, the authority of God's angels over the affairs of nations is asserted (see chap. 10).

Nebuchadnezzar is reminded that "the most High ruleth in the kingdom of men." This truth is affirmed throughout the Bible, and this verse is one more reminder that God reigns. If rebellion exists it is temporary and only by God's permission. If there is ignorance of Him, that too will in time be corrected. "There is no power but of God: the powers that be are ordained of God" (Rom. 13:1).

But God has made men his "vicegerents" to rule in His place. To use Nebuchadnezzar's words, He "giveth it to whomsoever he will." This, of course, has its bright side. Human government is necessary, not only to prevent violence and to secure physical safety but to "promote domestic tranquillity" and to secure the "general welfare" (see Rom. 13; Gen. 9:1-6; 1 Tim. 2:1-3).

Further, it is to be noted that God "setteth up over it [that is, the kingdom of men] the basest of men." Basest here likely means humblest, most base-born. To keep man in his place God has raised up even the most low-born to become kings.

5. The King's Appeal

> This dream I king Nebuchadnezzar have seen. Now thou, O Belteshazzar, declare the interpretation thereof, forasmuch as all the wise men of my kingdom are not able to make known unto me the interpretation: but thou art able; for the spirit of the holy gods is in thee (Dan. 4:18).

This appeal, in spite of all the fine things the king says about Daniel's God at the end of the chapter, is still the appeal of a pagan worshiper of many gods. He thinks the source of Daniel's wisdom is the presence of "the spirit of the holy gods" in him. The form of the words "holy gods" in the original Aramaic makes it clear that he is not referring to the one true God whose name *Elohim* (Aram. Elohin) is plural. He addresses Daniel by his pagan Babylonian Bel-honoring name, and obviously had called on his other counselors first.

III. INTERPRETATION OF THE DREAM
(Dan. 4:19-27)

It is worthy of note that God's man was quite unhurried about producing an answer to the king. The interpretation had to wait for the moving of the Spirit of God upon the mind of the prophet. The Spirit of God will not be subject either to authorities or to coercion. Daniel was "astonied for one hour," that is, for a period of time. During this time "his thoughts troubled him." This was not because he was fearful, but because the sad message brought about a measure of reluctance to deliver it.

1. An Ominous Hint

> ... Belteshazzar answered and said, My lord, the dream be to them that hate thee, and the interpretation thereof to thine enemies (Dan. 4:19).

The king had said in effect, "Speak up Daniel!" And now Daniel did just that. His first words were to the effect that Nebuchadnezzar would get no immediate comfort from the interpretation, but that his enemies and detractors would. Again we understand that the king had intuitively recognized bad news in his dream and why Daniel had been hesitant to relate the interpretation in the king's presence. When later at verse 25 it is said that, "They shall drive thee," and so forth, it is to be understood that "they" are these enemies within the king's own administration who were happy to demote him. Perhaps it was the loyalty of Daniel and others like him that prevented worse from happening to the king.

2. Interpretation of the Tree

> The tree that thou sawest, which grew, and was strong, whose height reached unto the heaven, and the sight thereof to all the earth; whose leaves were fair, and the fruit thereof much, and in it was meat for all; under which the beasts of the field dwelt, and upon whose branches the fowls of the heaven had their habitation: it is thou, O king, that art grown and become strong: for thy greatness is grown, and reacheth unto heaven, and thy dominion to the end of the earth (Dan. 4:20-22).

The tree is the king reigning in his kingdom and pride. Daniel's recapitulation of the king's dream is almost exactly that which Nebuchadnezzar had related. Having thus assured the king he knew all about the dream he came straight to the point, and this without either fear or harshness.

3. Interpretation of the Watcher

And whereas the king saw a watcher and an holy one coming down from heaven, and saying, Hew the tree down, and destroy it; yet leave the stump of the roots thereof in the earth, even with a band of iron and brass, in the tender grass of the field; and let it be wet with the dew of heaven, and let his portion be with the beasts of the field, till seven times pass over him. This is the interpretation, O king, and this is the decree of the most High, which is come upon my lord the king (Dan. 4:23-24).

Most of this is repetition of what the king had already said. But there is one most important addition by way of interpretation! The decree which in Nebuchadnezzar's recital had been attributed to the angelic watcher is here said to be "of the most High." Nebuchadnezzar was to know that no puny Babylonian deity was to be in charge of these disasters. Neither were they to come at the instigation of the gods of any foreign enemies. Rather these angelic watchers are messengers of the sovereign Lord and Creator of the entire universe, God Most High, identical with Daniel's God. It may be regarded as still another road sign leading the king away from his polytheistic faith. In Nebuchadnezzar's mouth the expression "God most high" means that among the many high gods, Daniel's is the highest. But in Daniel's, and it is he who speaks here, it means there is one God and He is supremely exalted, high over all His vast creation.

4. Interpretation of the Decree

That they shall drive thee from men, and thy dwelling shall be with the beasts of the field, and they shall make thee to eat grass as oxen, and they shall wet thee with the dew of heaven, and seven times shall pass over thee, till thou know that the most High ruleth in the kingdom of men, and giveth it to whomsoever he will. And whereas they commanded to leave the stump of the tree roots; thy kingdom shall be sure unto thee, after that thou shalt have known that the heavens do rule (Dan. 4:25-26).

The decree is interpreted to predict a period of unpleasant humbling experiences for the king during which he would learn to acknowledge the sovereign rule of God, following which the king would be restored to his former happy state.

"They shall drive thee from men." Nebuchadnezzar was a son of the great and lordly Nabopolassar, himself of a noble Chaldean family. It was this Nabopolassar who had asserted the independence of Babylon from the Assyrians in about 625 B.C. and a dozen years later had been a major force in effecting the destruction of Nineveh, the Assyrian capital. Nebuchadnezzar had fought and won great battles, had shown himself to be an intellectual and generally progressive monarch. His capital city, Babylon, bore the marks of his greatness. To have been told that he was to be demoted from aristocrat to peasant, from lord of Babylon to be one of its street cleaners would have been bad enough, but to be driven even from human association was utterly devastating to his self-esteem.

"Thy dwelling shall be with the beasts of the field" where his food would be from their pastures, mangers, and troughs. He was to lose all human dignity. "A man's pride shall bring him low" (Prov. 29:23)—and Nebuchadnezzar would learn just how low!

"Till thou know that the most High ruleth." God was dealing with Nebuchadnezzar in grace rather than in penal judgment. It was to teach rather than to exact punishment that God was to bring these things to Nebuchadnezzar. If the king had been willing to reflect on the fate of his neighbor nations, he might have been spared this painful lesson. At a time not more than a few months or years removed, Ezekiel, another Jewish prophet in exile, was spelling out the lesson for the benefit of the Pharaoh of Egypt (see Ezek. 30:20–31:18).

"Thy kingdom shall be sure unto thee." This was somewhat reassuring to the king. He was to be "cast down, but not forever." When God chastens for gracious purposes "the latter end," as with Job, is always "more than his beginning" (Job 42:12).

"After that thou shalt have known that the heavens do rule." This is about as near as the Old Testament level of revelation can come to Romans 10:9 ("that if thou shalt confess with thy mouth the Lord Jesus") and to Philippians 2:11 ("that every tongue should confess that Jesus Christ is Lord"). Whether or not Nebuchadnezzar came to true heart confession (Rom. 10:10), it remains true that to acknowledge that "the heavens" (God) is Lord is the heart of saving faith.

5. The Advice of Daniel (Dan. 4:27)

Daniel's words of advice are quite like other Old Testament calls to sincere repentance, mentioning the outward marks or evidences rather than the inward change behind them (see Joel 1:8, 14; 2:17-18). Yet those prophets believed there should be a rending of the hearts as well as of the garments (cf. Joel 2:13), and we may be sure that Daniel did the same.

Perhaps there had been much personal impurity ("sins") which needed to be broken up by truly right living. The king's oppressive treatment of his subjects ("iniquities") needed to be replaced by showing mercy to them. At any rate he was to put his change of heart on display! It is ever so.

IV. FULFILLMENT OF THE DREAM (Dan. 4:28-33)

> At the end of twelve months he walked in the palace of the kingdom of Babylon (Dan. 4:29).

Josephus, the famous first century Jewish historian, has written of Nebuchadnezzar that he built a new palace beside that of his father. The excavation of Babylon in the past century has quite fully authenticated Nebuchadnezzar's building activity. This is seen especially in the construction of an enormous palace on which was probably super-added the hanging gardens. Here in the midst of trees like the ones he loved in Lebanon and like the one of his dream of a year before the fulfillment took place.

> The king spake, and said, Is not this great Babylon, that I have built for the house of the kingdom by the might of my power,

and for the honour of my majesty? (Dan. 4:30).

As a matter of fact, everything the king claimed for his city here is quite strictly true. He could see stretching out endlessly a great street for religious processions. He had rebuilt it. There were new gates which he had built. There were several palaces and many temples, to say nothing of the miles of walls. "He also rebuilt the old city, and added another to it on the outside, and so far restored Babylon, that none who should besiege it afterwards might have it in their power to divert the river, so as to facilitate an entrance into it; and this he did by building three walls about the inner city, and three about the outer" (Josephus).

Suddenly, without any further indication, "While the word was in the king's mouth," a voice from heaven declared that all the things prophesied by Daniel would immediately take place.

Commentators in general agree that some form of insanity overtook the unhappy king. Pagan people have frequently supposed the insane to be actually indwelt by the person or god whom the insane person is believing himself to be. They, therefore, have been sometimes treated with a great deal of deference and respect. If this is the case with Nebuchadnezzar, he may very well have been placed in one of the city parks with other zoological "specimens" to carry on as he pleased. There the symptoms and characteristics so simply described in verse 33 could have developed. Stranger things than this have happened. There is no reason to doubt the story.

That the events described had something to do with a loss of mental powers is made certain by the fact that they came to an end by the return of the king's understanding (v. 34).

V. CONCLUSION: RESTORATION OF THE KING
(Dan. 4:34-37)

The length of the period, "seven times," cannot be specified. Likely it was seven years, though this is not certain. Perhaps seven is intended (Calvin) only as a perfect number to mean "long enough."

An important psychological fact is that the king heard a voice from heaven and likely directed his eyes in that direction at the onset of his insanity. After the passage of "seven times," he probably again looked toward heaven, as if taking up where he left off, to receive from heaven a return of understanding.

The results of the king's chastening experience are clearly seen in the praise, confession and testimony displayed in this portion.

Taking the evil of sinful human pride as the theme of this chapter, its development can be seen clearly as follows.

There is first the *root of sinful pride* (vv. 1-28). This was twofold: a sense of great personal accomplishment unmixed with any sense of dependence upon God and personal self-exaltation (see especially vv. 4, 10-11).

There is in the second place the *essence of sinful pride* (vv. 29-30). It consisted mainly in taking to one's self honors rightly belonging to another. It was God who had delivered to the king the goods and powers by which he built this city. Nebuchadnezzar gave God no credit.

In the third place, there is the *result of sinful pride* (vv. 31-33). Not only was there the abasement involved, as spelled out by such passages as Proverbs 16:18 and 29:23, but specifically insanity. Sin of any sort when engaged in without restraint is a kind of insanity (cf. the case of the Prodigal Son who returned only when he "came to himself," Luke 15:17).

In the fourth place, there is the *cure for sinful pride* (vv. 34-36) in a return to reason and to God. Nothing is more reasonable than the Gospel, even though the world in its wisdom does not know it. Dedication to God in Christian living is a "reasonable service" (Rom. 12:1-2).

Daniel 5

Belshazzar's Feast:

A Lesson in Sin and Its Fruits

I. Pleasure, the Pursuit of Belshazzar's Feast (Dan. 5:1-4)

II. A Portent, God's Contribution to Balshazzar's Feast (Dan. 5:5-6)

III. Perplexity, the Effect of This Visitation at Belshazzar's Feast (Dan. 5:7-9)

IV. Pronouncement of Doom, Daniel's Contribution to Belshazzar's Feast (Dan. 5:10-29)

V. Punishment, the End of the Feast of Belshazzar (Dan. 5:30-31)

Even a hasty reading of this chapter is sufficient to show the discerning reader that the chief purpose of Daniel is not to recite history but to teach spiritual truth. The demands of history are quite fully met by the first verse and last two verses—the last Chaldean king was killed by an opposing force of Medes and Persians with a Median king named Darius becoming the new monarch. The main part of the chapter, however, reports the foolish and wicked pursuit of sinful thrills and pleasures on the part of Belshazzar.

When the story of this chapter opens before us, 70 years have passed since the events of chapter 1. Dissimulation and assassination have actually changed the dynasties twice in Babylon, though a measure of continuity with the great Nebuchadnezzar by marriages has been attempted. The union of two peoples, the Persians to the east of Babylon and the Medes to the east and north, under the Persian prince, Cyrus, had recently created a formidable enemy in the neighborhood. A doughty warrior like Nabopolassar, the founder of the empire, or a bold and resourceful king like Nebuchadnezzar, might have been equal to the times. But neither they nor any others like them were to be found in Babylon.

The passing over of the supposedly important affairs of nations and their kings and potentates by the Bible in favor of full report of small incidents exemplifying important spiritual principles deserves to be pondered. The lesson and lecture on the follies of pride and sinful pleasure are important to God and to His people. The fall of a sparrow or the wail of a neglected child may be more important to Him and to us than the fall of a government or party or the diplomatic exchanges of great nations.

I. PLEASURE, THE PURSUIT OF BELSHAZZAR'S FEAST (Dan. 5:1-4)

Belshazzar the king made a great feast to a thousand of his lords, and drank wine before the thousand. Belshazzar, whiles he tasted the wine, commanded to bring the golden and silver vessels which his father Nebuchadnezzar had taken out of the temple which was in Jerusalem; that the king, and his princes, his wives, and his concubines, might drink therein. Then they brought the golden vessels that were taken out of the temple of the house of God which was at Jerusalem; and the king, and his princes, his wives, and his concubines, drank in them. They drank wine, and praised the gods of gold, and of silver, of brass, of iron, of wood, and of stone (Dan. 5:1-4).

There are at least four sad facts to be observed about the sinful pursuit of pleasure by the stupid young king and his silly guests.

1. It was *sinfully sensual.* Anything in the ancient pagan world that would be called a "great feast" would have been thus. We have no direct detailed reports of the feasts in Babylon comparable to those of the ancient Greeks and Romans, but it is safe to say that what was true in pagan Greece and Rome was true here also. There would have been overeating—actual gorging with food. When capacity to eat was exhausted, emetics were sometimes taken to enable the revelers to disgorge their food and start in all over again.

One by one they drank themselves to the floors and under the tables. Add to this feast of Belshazzar the overtones of sexuality provided by the presence of the wives and concubines—all drinking wine—and the details furnished by the reader's imagination are probably no worse than the true facts of the case.

2. It was *unrestrained.* All the bars were down. That the king "drank wine before the thousands" (v. 1) must be interpreted in the light of court procedures and royal protocol known to have prevailed in the ancient East. Kings and queens were cloistered, especially among the Persians, and probably no less among the Babylonians. Curtains shut them off from view at almost all occasions—and especially at feasts.

Proper decorum and pure morality do not necessarily require the negation or repression of natural appetites and desires. But they do certainly require their control and lawful direction. It was not the eating and drinking in themselves that were sinful and which were working the young king's destruction. It was rather his lack of temperate self-control.

3. It was *sacrilegious.* Under the inspiration of the wine Belshazzar sent for the "golden and silver vessels which his father Nebuchadnezzar had taken out of the temple which was in Jerusalem." This was done in order to have something special by way of table service for his feast. This order had not been given in his sober hours when the feast was being prepared. He would not have dared to do it then.

It should be added that for Nebuchadnezzar to remove the vessels from the Jerusalem temple as an act of war was according to the accepted practices of the time, and was not regarded as sacrilegious. For Belshazzar to remove them in a drinking bout *was* sacrilegious.

4. It was *stupid.* According to an old proverb, "Whom the gods would destroy they first make mad." Archaeology and ancient history join in reporting just how stupid the whole feast was and just how foolish the young king was. Let us take a look at the local circumstances in relation to biblical prophecy.

Sometime before the Persians became "top dogs" in the Medo-Persian combination, Jeremiah had prophesied that Babylon would be attacked by an invader from the north (cf. Jer. 50:3, 9) whom he identified with "the kings of the Medes" (cf. Jer. 51:11, 28). Babylon is described in the prophecy as stocked with provisions and protected by great towering forts, high broad walls and mighty gates (cf. Jer. 51:53, 58). She would, however, be taken by a trick or snare (cf. Jer. 50:24) connected with drying up of certain water channels (51:36 "I will dry up her sea, and make her springs dry"). The "passages are stopped" (that is, the ferries that joined the streets in lieu of bridges from one side of the Euphrates to the other, Jer. 51:32), the soldiers were to be taken by surprise, and the reeds were to be burned. Jeremiah further predicted that this would be accomplished while a great feast was going on in Babylon (cf. Jer. 5:39).

Some 75 years after Cyrus conquered Babylon, Herodotos visited the place and wrote his history. According to this

Greek historian Cyrus neared the city in the spring of the year (539 B.C.). After being defeated in the field by Cyrus, the Babylonians retired behind their walls. "Here they shut themselves up," says Herodotos, "and made light of his siege, having laid in store of provisions for many years in preparation against this attack [cf. Dan. 4:12, Jer. 50:26]; for when they saw Cyrus conquering nation after nation, they were convinced that he would never stop, and that their turn would come."

Herodotos' story continues by relating how Cyrus took the city, in spite of its fortifications and supplies, by a strategem. A portion of his army he stationed at the point where the Euphrates entered the city on the upper side. Another force he set at the spot where the river emerged from the city with orders to both parties to march into the town by way of the riverbed as soon as it should become shallow enough. Then he retired with a third part of the troops to a point up the river where there was a marshy basin formerly used to divert the river waters while the quay walls within the city had been lined with brick. On the very night of Balshazzar's feast this army diverted the waters of Euphrates into this reservoir.

It is plain that during the very hours of Belshazzar's ill-timed feast the armies of the Persians were stealthily moving through the riverbed toward the inner gates opening on that river. By the time Daniel came to the palace they were likely moving toward that palace. Never in the annals of history was anything more stupid than the feast of Belshazzar.

II. A PORTENT, GOD'S CONTRIBUTION TO BELSHAZZAR'S FEAST (Dan. 5:5-6)

In the same hour came forth fingers of a man's hand, and wrote over against the candlestick upon the plaster of the wall of the king's palace: and the king saw the part of the hand that wrote. Then the king's countenance was changed, and his thoughts troubled him, so that the joints of his loins were loosed, and his knees smote one against another (Dan. 5:5-6).

These two verses have made such an impression on the entire world that they have given the world a commonly understood expression in the words, "the handwriting on the wall." These words and the mysterious hand that wrote them were a divine portent, that is, a supernatural sign, or omen—not a warning of coming calamity to enable the observer to escape, but rather simply to notify him that doom is certain.

Daniel 5:5 *Over against the candlestick.* The word for candlestick used here appears nowhere else. There are no lexicographical sources from which to obtain an exact meaning. An ancient Greek translation (Theodotion) renders it *lampos,* which, as one would expect, means lamp or lantern. It would likely have been a large candelabrum containing many small lamps.

1. The sign came *suddenly*—"in the same hour." That is, while the belching and slobbering crowd of noble revelers were sopping up their wine out of the holy vessels of Jehovah's temple they received their divine bill of attainder.

2. The sign was *mysterious,* for there "came forth fingers of a man's hand, and wrote," and "the king saw the part of the hand that wrote" (v. 5). The word for hand in Aramaic and Hebrew is not as specific as ours, for it sometimes evidently was used to refer to the entire forearm. Therefore, qualifying words are used to make it clear that it was only the extremity of the arm that appeared. The word in verse 5 rendered "part" is the usual word for palm of the hand. The same is the case in verse 24. This joined with the mention of the "fingers of a man's hand" makes it clear that it was the part of the arm below the wrist which appeared.

3. It was *ruthless,* for the part of the hand that wrote left a new inscription "over against the candlestick upon the plaster of the wall of the king's palace." Excavators have uncovered that palace and have exposed portions of the ancient walls where remnants of the white gypsum with which they were once covered could be seen. The great central room of the palace, half the size of a football field, was joined by the throne room which itself was over 50 yards long and a third

as much in width.

If the usual customs of antiquity prevailed, the walls were decorated with murals and inscriptions celebrating the victories and excellencies of the realm. Their gods and goddesses ("which see not, nor hear, nor know," v. 23) would have been glorified in those representations, too. Over this proud and boastful display, in full glare of the "candlestick" (that is, a prominent candelabrum or lampstand), God wrote His own verdict concerning the empire and its stupid young king.

4. It was *terrifying,* for "the king saw.... Then the king's countenance was changed, and ... the joints of his loins were loosed, and his knees smote one against another" (v. 6). Everything about the situation inclined toward such an effect upon even the stoutest hearts and the most sober minds present. There were the dozens of open, saucer-like lamps distributed about the hall, each sending a thin column of smoke toward the ceiling in addition to the feeble light it cast about the room. Into the murky sodden atmosphere came the sudden apparition. No wonder the king's knees knocked together!

III. PERPLEXITY, THE EFFECT OF THIS VISITATION AT BELSHAZZAR'S FEAST (Dan. 5:7-9)

> The king cried aloud to bring in the astrologers, the Chaldeans, and the soothsayers. And the king spake, and said to the wise men of Babylon, Whosoever shall read this writing, and shew me the interpretation thereof, shall be clothed with scarlet, and have a chain of gold about his neck, and shall be the third ruler in the kingdom. Then came in all the king's wise men: but they could not read the writing, nor make known to the king the interpretation thereof. Then was king Belshazzar greatly troubled, and his countenance was changed in him, and his lords were astonied (Dan. 5:7-9).

A few items call for explanation and interpretation before continuing.

The "scarlet" with which the interpreter of the writing was to be clothed should be translated "purple." Purple was the color of royalty among Persians, Medes, and Greeks, and likely among Babylonians also. Artistic remains of that part of the ancient world show that golden chains were associated with high offices of government.

The expression "third ruler" is uncertain of meaning. There is small doubt that the root of the word is the usual Aramaic word for "three," but according to language authorities this form of the word could easily mean something like adjutant or simply "officer." The word "lord" used of a king's adjutant in 2 Kings 7:2 and elsewhere is the Hebrew word *shalish* meaning literally, third. So "third ruler" may be a reminiscence of the name of an officer in the Babylonian government. On the other hand, it may mean literally "third ruler."

The immediate urgent cry for a solution to the mystery of the supernatural writing shows there was a sudden end to all the merrymaking in the banquet hall, and that more than anything else he had ever wanted, King Belshazzar wanted to know what that writing meant. The inducements offered were such as would have called forth the best efforts of anyone qualified to try.

But no one came up with a solution to the riddle. The statement that "his lords were perplexed" (ASV) shows there was a general feeling of helplessness and bafflement about the whole affair.

IV. PRONOUNCEMENT OF DOOM, DANIEL'S CONTRIBUTION TO BELSHAZZAR'S FEAST (Dan. 5:10-29)

1. The Queen-Mother's Visit and Suggestion (Dan. 5:10-12).

Now the queen, by reason of the words of the king and his lords, came into the banquet house: and the queen spake and said, O king, live for ever: let not thy thoughts trouble thee, nor let thy countenance be changed: There is a man in thy kingdom, in whom is the spirit of the holy gods; and in the days of thy father light and understanding and wisdom, like the wisdom of the gods, was found in him; whom the king Nebuchadnezzar thy father, the king, I say, thy father, made master of the magicians, astrologers, Chaldeans, and soothsayers; forasmuch as an excellent spirit, and knowledge, and understanding, interpreting of dreams, and shewing of hard sentences, and dissolving of doubts, were found in the same Daniel, whom the king named Belteshazzar: now let Daniel be called, and he will shew the interpretation (Dan. 5:10-12).

Who is this latecomer to the banquet, called "the queen"? It is clear she was not the king's wife. The wives were already there, and besides, she speaks as an older person who remembered better days of long ago. Furthermore, in the households of the polygamous kings of antiquity it was usually the king's mother, or even grandmother, who was the "grand lady" or "queen of the realm." This queen could have been the wife of Nabonidus, Belshazzar's father. There is also the possibility that she may have been a daughter of Nebuchadnezzar—in which case Belshazzar would have been Nebuchadnezzar's grandson. There is still another possibility that she had been a young wife of Nebuchadnezzar who had been married to Nabonidus to give his throne greater prestige and power. She is supposed by some, not without evidence, to have been none other than a famous "Nitocris" who was an ambitious and resourceful person.

How could the queen refer to Nebuchadnezzar as "thy father"? Critics of a former generation made great sport of this supposed inaccuracy—it being well known that several kings had reigned between the time of Nebuchadnezzar and this night. Even so, the death of Nebuchadnezzar had taken place less than 25 years before, and that famous king could, therefore, have been his father. The ancients of the Near East, however, used the word "father" of a number of relationships other than that of immediate male progenitor. But, the view that seems to fit the materials furnished by archaeology is that Belshazzar was son of Nebuchadnezzar in a legal sense only. It was, however, a matter of court etiquette to call Belshazzar son of Nebuchadnezzar. Notice how punctilious the aged queen was about it. Three times in verse 11 she refers to Nebuchadnezzar as Belshazzar's father. Once in verse 13 Belshazzar claims Nebuchadnezzar as his father, and once in verse 22 Daniel calls Belshazzar Nebuchadnezzar's son. These multiplied occurrences make it clear that whatever the basis may have been for it, it was a matter of court etiquette to refer to Belshazzar as son of Nebuchadnezzar.

How Daniel's former reputation could have been either ignored or forgotten between the days of Nebuchadnezzar and those of Belshazzar some 25 years later is not hard to suppose. He was, after all, a foreigner and of a captive nation. He had, moreover, repeatedly predicted the downfall of Babylonian power under the successors of Nebuchadnezzar which would have made him unpopular. And, inasmuch as men tend to forget that which is inconvenient or unpleasant to remember, it is not hard to believe that Belshazzar simply hadn't thought of calling him in. It is doubtful if he was still master of the wise men of Babylon, for he would have been in the neighborhood of 85 years of age by the time of this fateful night.

2. The Entrance of Daniel (Dan. 5:13-16).

The impression made upon the king and his crowd by the entrance of the venerable and saintly Daniel would have been quieting. There is every evidence of respect in the king's words.

How completely men of worldly interests misunderstand the things which move better people is exemplified here. "Clothed with purple ... a chain of gold about his neck ... third ruler in the kingdom"—what did they, what *could* they mean to this hoary-headed old man? He had started life in the Holy Land, soon thereafter to become a captive. He had seen kings and realms come and go. Through it all he had lived a quiet, godly, useful life with faith toward God and respect for his fellow man.

3. The Message of Daniel (Dan. 5:17-24).

> Then Daniel answered and said before the king, Let thy gifts be to thyself, and give thy rewards to another; yet I will read the writing unto the king, and make known to him the interpretation (Dan. 5:17).

There is a certain sharpness about these words. If the king's conduct had been offensive to God it had been so to Daniel, also. Daniel, therefore, while speaking with proper respect, could not use the customary flattering encomiums when addressing their king. Neither could he in good grace accept the gifts.

The main part of Daniel's message to the king was a simple review of the story of chapter 4; Nebuchadnezzar's pride and the harsh discipline he received from God to make him humble. Nebuchadnezzar, however, was restored to his kingly power when he had learned his lesson. What about Belshazzar?

Before telling the king just what his fate would be and before interpreting the mysterious writing on the wall, Daniel stated the sins charged against Belshazzar. They were four. (1) In the first place *he had refused to acknowledge the divine revelation in the experience of Nebuchadnezzar:* "thou his son, O Belshazzar, hast not humbled thine heart, though thou knewest all this" (v. 22). Old men are not granted the excuses for their sins that are given youths—oldsters should profit by years of experience and observation.

(2) In the second place, *he, too, had committed the horrid sin of pride*—"thou hast lifted up thyself against the Lord of heaven" (v. 23). Isaiah had prophesied "against the king of Babylon" (Isa. 14:4), "For thou hast said in thine heart, I will ascend into heaven, I will exalt my throne above the stars of God . . . I will ascend above the heights of the clouds; I will be like the most High. Yet thou shalt be brought down . . . " (Isa. 14:13-15). Is it perhaps this Belshazzar whom Isaiah had in mind? This part of the prophecy, at least, fits him.

(3) In the third place, *he had engaged in a peculiarly offensive idolatry,* a sacrilegious idolatry that was specifically insulting to the Lord (see v. 23). God had judged His own Jewish people with destruction of their nation precisely be-

cause they had mixed idolatry with their worship of Him. They had committed sacrilege. This Gentile reprobate could not expect to be spared for committing the same sin.

(4) Finally, Belshazzar *had refused to carry out the true purpose of his own and every other man's existence—to glorify God*—"and the God in whose hand thy breath is, and whose are all thy ways, hast thou not glorified" (v. 23). All the fierce wrath of God upon idolatrous self-will worship described in Paul's mighty words of Romans 1:28-32 is here focused upon Belshazzar. Read it and tremble.

Terrible must be the fate of Belshazzar!

4. Interpretation of the Handwriting by Daniel (Dan. 5:25-28)

And this is the writing that was written, MENE, MENE, TEKEL, UPHARSIN (Dan. 5:25).

The reader of the English Bible, or any other translation for that matter, has no way of knowing that these three words (MENE is repeated) were common everyday terms in the Aramaic language. Aramaic is the language of this portion of the Book of Daniel. It was likewise a common language on the streets and in the marts and courts of Babylon. An explanation is in order.

All ancient Semitic languages, of which Hebrew, Aramaic, and Babylonian were examples, were written without vowel marks. The alphabet employed for Hebrew and Aramaic had capital letters only. Now, holding in mind that Aramaic was written from right to left it would have appeared on the wall as

$$\longleftarrow$$
$$\text{SRP} \quad \text{LQT} \quad \text{NM} \quad \text{NM}$$

If we reverse it left to right according to our method of writing it would appear as

$$\longrightarrow$$
$$\text{MN} \quad \text{MN} \quad \text{TQL} \quad \text{PRS}$$

With no context to guide the reader they were incomprehensible. They could have been read as names of weights or coins, for example: a mina, a mina, a shekel, a peres; like a dollar, a dollar, a dime, and a penny; or a pound, a pound, a shilling, a penny. If, as seems unlikely, they were written in the Babylonian wedge-shaped characters, some of which were signs for syllables that served also as ideograms, then it was even more complicated. Proceeding on the near certainty that it was Aramaic, it should be observed that with the vowels supplied and printed in our Bibles, the words would be simply translated: "counted, counted, weighed, divided." But these words have no subject or object supplied—thus still need for an interpreter. Except that the last word sounded like Persia, there was almost no suggestion that it was connected with a victory by the enemy.

> This is the interpretation of the thing: MENE; God hath numbered thy kingdom, and finished it (Dan. 5:26).

Better, read: "God hath numbered thy *reign*." The number of days during which Belshazzar might reign was fixed by God and now at a complete end. Belshazzar, the jig is up!

> TEKEL; Thou art weighed in the balances, and art found wanting (Dan. 5:27).

A cross-arm balanced on a post at midpoint with trays suspended from the ends by chains or cords, like the scales seen on display in some drugstores, is the picture. There is a certain breath-stopping expectancy about the process of weighing by this method. The standard weight is set on one tray; the substance to be weighed, on the other. If there is enough of the substance in question poured or set on to equal exactly the mass of weight on the other platter the weight is raised as the beam adjusts itself to level. If not, then the substance is not heavy enough. The weight never rises. In the eternal scales of the judgment of God Belshazzar has been weighed in God's scales but he didn't move the beam. He had failed as a king.

> PERES; Thy kingdom is divided, and given to the Medes and Persians (Dan. 5:28).

UPHARSIN of verse 25 is replaced by PERES here. The explanation is as follows: "U" was possibly not part of the inscription at all. It is the Aramaic word for "and"—supplied by Daniel in reporting. "P" in Hebrew and Aramaic becomes "PH" or "F" after a vowel, hence the change from <u>PH</u>ARSIN to <u>P</u>ERES. The dropping of "in" is merely a change from plural to singular. The vowel changes are incidental to the other changes.

The plural form of the word suggests that "*they* shall be divided," that is, the various parts of the empire will be separated again. Jeremiah prophesied this (cf. Jer. 51:44). The word PERES was also a grim pun on the word "Paras" or Persia. (Another ancient name of the country is Aran.)

There is another grim suggestion in the tenses: "*hath* numbered . . . *art* weighed . . . *is* divided" and so forth, placing the judgments and decisions in the past. Even as Daniel pronounced the words the city had fallen and Belshazzar's executioners were on their way.

In the face of all this the foolish and unrepentant king still could not think it was really true that his time was up, for he went ahead to confer on Daniel the promised rewards as though he were still master of the proudest realm of earth.

V. PUNISHMENT, THE END OF THE FEAST OF BELSHAZZAR (Dan. 5:30-31)

The punishment was no less startling in its sudden execution than the apparition of the fingers writing the inscription had been. Both were in just proportion to the rashness of the king in his sacrilegious use of the vessels of the Lord.

The reader who knows his Bible cannot help but be impressed with the demonstration herein of the certainty of God's promises and providence. Isaiah had prophesied that God would raise up one Cyrus from the east to "dry up the rivers" (Euphrates and Tigris), in figure, in order that His people, the Jews might return to their land, reestablish their commonwealth, and rebuild their temple (see Isa. 40–45, especially 44:24–45:4). Now, not far away stands this very Cyrus while his general Darius invests and takes over the city. Sixty-some years before Daniel had prophesied first of the coming of the Medes and Persians, a "kingdom inferior" (Dan. 2:39), and again just a few years later had repeated it (cf. chap. 7, v. 1), to replace the Chaldeans as masters of the world. This chapter tells us exactly how it all came to pass.

In a different, but quite as impressive manner, the man who knows little of God's Word, the Bible, who may not even acknowledge the Saviour, should see in the experiences of Daniel and Belshazzar something of the importance of knowing God in a saving way, and of bringing his life into obedient relationship to Him. Life moves on inexorably toward its end. Life is a time of sowing. At its end one will, if he has sown to the Spirit, reap life everlasting. If one has sown to the flesh, he shall of the flesh reap corruption. God will render "to them who by patient continuance in well-doing seek for glory and honour and immortality, eternal life: but unto them that are contentious, and do not obey the truth, but obey unrighteousness, indignation and wrath, tribulation and anguish . . ." (Rom. 2:7-9).

Let us not in that day hear: "Weighed in the balances and found wanting." But rather with sins forgiven by the grace of God through the blood of Christ, may we hear Christ, Himself, supreme judge, say: "Enter thou into the joy of thy Lord."

6

Daniel 6

Daniel in the Lions' Den:

A Message of Faith and Prayer

I. The Position of Daniel (Dan. 6:1-3)

II. The Plot against Daniel (Dan. 6:4-9)

III. The Prayer of Daniel (Dan. 6:10-11)

IV. The Success of the Plot against Daniel (Dan. 6:11-17)

V. God's Answer to Daniel's Prayer (Dan. 6:17-28)

The message concerning faith and prayer conveyed by this chapter has its setting in a story of religious persecution. The story tells of an attempt to destroy a good man by finding an "occasion against" him in connection with the "law of his God." This report is rendered specially lucid because it relates to Daniel, the author of the book.

Persecution of the worshipers of God is an old, old story. It starts with the murder of Abel, whose brother Cain hated him when Abel's works showed him up for the spiritual fraud he was (cf. I John 3:12). It continues throughout the Old Testament narratives of the ministry of God's servants. So pronounced was the tendency of ancient Israel to persecute the prophets that Jesus could speak of Jerusalem as "thou that killest the prophets, and stonest them which are sent unto thee" (Matt. 23:37, vv. 33-36).

The persecution of Christians is an issue of our time! Who knows how many of them have died in Russia? In China? Nobody knows when some new Hitler or Stalin or Mao or Iddi Amin may arise to carry off more.

Our resources in such a time are the same as Daniel's were. Let us see what they are.

I. THE POSITION OF DANIEL (Dan. 6:1-3)

It pleased Darius to set over the kingdom an hundred and twenty princes, which should be over the whole kingdom (Dan. 6:1).

To the present moment no prominent person named Darius has turned up in the known inscriptions relating to the fall of Babylon. This need not embarrass the Bible believer at all. In the first place, remember that the situation is not dissimilar to that concerning Belshazzar 100 years ago. The respectability of the fifth chapter account of him is now thoroughly established to the satisfaction even of the critics. The same may yet take place with regard to Darius. In the second place, it was a common thing in antiquity for kings to have two names, frequently taking a new name at their royal accession. The kings of Israel and Judah furnish many examples of this (for example, 2 Chron. 36:4, 8-9, Jer. 22:24). Cyrus himself might have had Darius as another name. What is more likely is that one of several other persons mentioned frequently in both the Greek histories and in the contemporary Babylonian temple records is the Darius of Daniel. Dr. John Whitcomb of Grace Theological Seminary (*Darius the Mede,* Eerdmans, 1958) has made a most convincing case for identifying him with *Gubaru* who ruled Babylon for a good while during and following 539 B.C. in the stead of his lord, Cyrus.

If this be the case, then the problem of Darius' kingdom has been cleared up. It has been pointed out by Daniel's detractors that a different division of Cyrus' realm from that of "an hundred and twenty princes" is reported in secular sources. But Daniel has no reference to what Cyrus did with the extensive dominions which we call the Medo-Persian Empire. Daniel, rather, has reference to what Gubaru (Darius) did with his large, but less extensive, dominions in and around the city of Babylon.

> And over these three presidents; of whom Daniel was first: that the princes might give accounts unto them, and the king should have no damage (Dan. 6:2)

"No damage," that is, no loss, makes it clear that the purpose of the king's new governmental structure was concerned mainly with financial matters instead of the administration of justice. These ancient monarchs had no conception of the administration of government "for the people"—to borrow the great emancipator's phrase. Government was for the king. Occasionally a benevolent man would arise to give the people something like fair treatment, but it was exceptional.

Darius is not to be criticized for taking steps to insure fiscal soundness to his realm. Any degree of national integrity, to say nothing of justice, will require fiscal soundness. No way will likely ever be found to spend a nation rich, nor to waste resources without resulting national poverty.

> Then this Daniel was preferred above the presidents and

princes, because an excellent spirit was in him; and the king thought to set him over the whole realm (Dan. 6:3).

The fact that Daniel was selected as one of the three indicates that he may have been already an international figure. Sixty-some years of distinguished public service in the greatest realm on earth would have made him that. Furthermore, it establishes as near certain that Daniel's activities on that last fateful night of Belshazzar had been reported to Darius.

There are several important truths suggested by these things. Does not the appointment of a man well past 80 years of age to high government office suggest the value of years where wisdom is necessary? That leadership abilities are the gift of God is suggested by the fact that "an excellent spirit was in him." The same expression at Daniel 5:12 clearly has reference to his gifts of wisdom. In that case, even the queen and the pagan king regard it as a divine gift.

Daniel's exaltation to high office in the new administration, and the proposed further promotion, were the occasion of new dangers. He was, after all, not only a carry-over from the hated Babylonians but a member of a captive people, the Hebrews. Such a man in such a position would almost inevitably be attacked by rivals among the conquering people. Add to this the peculiarity of Daniel's monotheistic faith and trouble becomes a near certainty.

II. THE PLOT AGAINST DANIEL (Dan. 6:4-9)

Then the presidents and princes sought to find occasion against Daniel concerning the kingdom; but they could find none occasion nor fault; forasmuch as he was faithful, neither was there any error or fault found in him (Dan. 6:4).

A very common situation was developing: envy driving men to attack a professional colleague more competent than themselves. Daniel had been wisely promoted to the position of the king's "prime minister"; the other princes and presidents being passed over. His superior moral and intellectual qualities apparently were well known.

Nothing is more true to the common experience of our fallen race than the proverb: "Wrath is cruel, and anger is outrageous; but who is able to stand before envy?" (Prov. 27:4). Daniel was in real danger. It is much to Daniel's credit, however, that no fault of any kind could be found in connection with his civil life and civic duties.

> Then said these men, we shall not find any occasion against this Daniel, except we find it against him concerning the law of his God (Dan. 6:5).

Daniel's danger lay not only in the high elevation for which his lord, King Darius, was responsible, but also in the fact his integrity guaranteed exactly how he would act in certain situations. His future conduct in a simple choice between right and wrong was predictable. In any contest of this sort the initial advantage always lies with the side of evil. So, these crooked politicians knew well that Daniel would not be disloyal to his God for any reason or for any consideration whether of gain or loss. Herein lay their advantage and Daniel's danger.

> Then these presidents and princes assembled together to the king, and said thus unto him, King Darius, live for ever. All the presidents of the kingdom, the governors, and the princes, the counsellors, and the captains, have consulted together to establish a royal statute, and to make a firm decree, that whosoever shall ask a petition of any God or man for thirty days, save of thee, O king, he shall be cast into the den of lions. Now, O king, establish the decree, and sign the writing, that it be not changed, according to the law of the Medes and Persians, which altereth not (Dan. 6:6-9).

The strength of this plan lay in taking advantage of the king's vanity. Their honorific manner of addressing him: "King Darius, live for ever" coupled with the vain self-praising proposal that the king actually assume divine honors were the sort of things which would appeal to a pagan king's vanity. Darius probably had been only a general of Cyrus up till his "being made" king of Babylon. And being past 62 years of age (cf. Dan. 5:31), he had waited long for the recognition of his military talents only recently acknowledged by his appointment, and accordingly had not many years in which to enjoy the glory.

Several matters call for at least brief attention. One is that a lie was involved in the plotters' speech. They said "all the presidents" had consulted together, whereas Daniel had not consulted with them.

Another is that the method of execution, by being fed to lions; whereas the fiery furnace was used by the Babylonians (chap. 3), is a truly authentic touch confirming the truth of the story. The ancient Persians of that time were Zoroastrians. Their religion, perpetuated today under the name of Parseeism ("Persianism"), held fire to be sacred. It would not be thought proper, therefore, that fire should be contaminated by corpses.

A further note is the sly remark of the plotters about Medo-Persian law—"which altereth not." It was this feature of their jurisprudence that made their plot workable and which effectively placed even the unhappy monarch at their disposal. This characteristic of the law, as we shall see, is a fulfillment of Daniel's words of chapter 2 about the future of human governments.

> Wherefore king Darius signed the writing and the decree (Dan. 6:9).

Actually the original says nothing of a "signing" of the document. Ancient kings used rotary seals pressed on clay or wax instead of our now customary signature. A literal translation which makes very awkward English is "the writing was written."

In three respects the king by the action reported here showed himself to be a poor ruler. 1) Personal *vanity*, about which we have previously spoken, is the worst trait displayed. 2) *Unfairness* to his appointed subordinates is seen in his failure to consult Daniel. His precipitous decision shows a kind of *impromptu judgment* most unfortunate in those whose decisions affect many people. These failures of Darius as king would be failures of any leader, in whatever capacity he might be.

III. THE PRAYER OF DANIEL (Dan. 6:10-11)

Before examining the prayer, a bit of reflection on just whose prayer it is should take place. Daniel is a man famous in his own day among fellow believers for his righteousness. God Himself shared in this popular estimate of him for, in God's message of destruction of Judah, He said, "Though these three men, Noah, Daniel, and Job, were in it, they should deliver but their own souls by their righteousness" (Ezek. 14:14). Furthermore, only a few years later, God's angel addressed Daniel: "O Daniel, a man greatly beloved" (Dan. 10:11). Such a man as this is worthy of close observation and emulation in whatever he does—but especially in a holy exercise like that of prayer.

> Now when Daniel knew that the writing was signed, he went into his house; and his windows being open in his chamber toward Jerusalem, he kneeled upon his knees three times a day, and prayed, and gave thanks before his God, as he did aforetime (Dan. 6:10).

The word for *house* is the ordinary word, but the word for chamber is a special word meaning *roof-chamber.* Such a roof-chamber would have been built upon some corner of the housetop or even on a specially constructed tower. To allow free circulation of air its sides would be really lattice windows. There are many scriptural references to such rooftop arrangements to provide relative privacy for prayer and meditation. In the case of Daniel's prayer room he had pushed back the frames of the lattice to provide free view toward Jerusalem several hundreds of miles to the west. The language appears to mean that Daniel had been leaving the windows open during the time of prayer, and now, when more complete privacy would have seemed cowardly, he did not close them.

Before entering this holy room with the expositor's spade of analysis let us look at the two facts which make it significant. They are first, the praying took place "when Daniel knew that the writing was signed," and second, it was prayer "as he did aforetime." The sublimity of holy, courageous faith that these words suggest cannot be explained; it can only be felt. The act of prayer was the only step Daniel took in the face of what he knew to be an inescapable trap.

A. Daniel's prayer was *courageous.* He prayed "when he knew that the writing was signed" which proscribed prayer to any god save the king an act of treason, making it punishable by death.

B. Daniel's prayer was *truly pious.* It was "pure religion and undefiled" (James 1:27). He did not go to the marketplace to make his prayer really a kind of political act. Neither did he send a note to the authorities announcing his intentions and then go home to pray. He simply "went into his house ... and prayed, and gave thanks before his God." There was no parade of religion. True piety does not care whether its exercises are observed or not.

C. Daniel's prayer was *according to the word of God.* This is especially important for our instruction and should accordingly be given careful and somewhat extended attention.

The captivity of Judah had been foreseen by God and announced by his prophets ahead of time, just as the replacement of judges by kings had been foreseen long before the days of Samuel and Saul. And just as God had provided guidance for the people after they should receive a king (cf. Deut. 17:14-20), so He provided guidance for them while they were in exile in foreign lands. Deuteronomy 28:36, and following, contain Moses' most specific portrayal of the anguish they would suffer in their captivities. These warnings were, like all biblical warnings to believers, deterrents to the sins thus to be punished. Knowing, however, that the warnings would not always be heeded, and that captivity would come, God gave instruction for them in their captivity. The best summary of

From Page 63, Book 1

it, coming from a prayer of King Solomon, is to be found in 2 Chronicles 6:36-39. This should be carefully studied to understand Daniel's actions.

Thus with full regard to what he knew and believed— Daniel prayed. I suggest there are at least seven or eight distinct elements involved in prayer according to the Word of God as exemplified by this man of God.

(1) It involved *faith* for, with his window opened toward Jerusalem, it was "toward their land, which thou gavest unto their fathers," howbeit, likewise "in the land of their captivity." His action involved confidence that the land guaranteed by formal covenant promise to Abraham and his descendants would truly be restored to them. As is to be seen in chapter 9, he even believed that he was living in the very days of its restoration. He did not come to prayer as a last resource supposing that "somehow" it might help. No! On the basis of God's promises he came expectantly (cf. James 1:6-7). "LET HIM ASK IN FAITH, NOTHING WAVERING"

Note also the remark in Daniel 6:23: *"because he believed [trusted] in his God."* It should be observed that this is not a part of Darius' speech. Neither is it merely a report of Daniel's feelings at the occasion. It is rather God's own opinion as to the reason for Daniel's deliverance, reported by Daniel as an author of Scripture.

(2) It involved *worship*, for this also is involved in the windows open toward Jerusalem. Solomon's language was, "toward the city which thou hast chosen." In the Mosaic epoch worship was not to be held just anywhere. It was to be at "the place which the Lord your God shall choose out of all your tribes to put his name there, even unto his habitation shall ye seek, and thither thou shalt come ... thither shall ye bring your ... offerings, and your sacrifices, and your tithes. ... And there ye shall eat before the Lord" (Deut. 12:5-7). By a series of remarkable miracles God had designated the city of Jerusalem and Mount Moriah, the site of the temple, as the place of His choosing (1 Chron. 11:4-9; 13:1-14;

15:25-29; 21:9-30; 2 Chron. 3:1-2; 5:1-14; 7:1-3). So, Daniel, recognizing that effectual prayer is only possible when respect is had to God in worship, directed his prayer toward the city of Jerusalem.

(3) Further involved in the direction of Daniel's prayer was the *ground of sacrificial blood atonement.* Prayer "toward the house ... built for thy name" was toward a temple whose main purpose was the perpetuation of a complicated, but necessary, ritual of blood atonement. Twice daily there were burnt-offerings for the welfare of the whole nation. Once a year there was the ritual of national atonement. At all times of the day there were individual sacrifices being made for the sins of conscience-stricken Israelites who came there to get right with their God. Access to God then was by blood. How joyously the New Testament reports the application to us! See Hebrews 10:19-22. This is the significance of our prayers "in Jesus' name."

(4) *Humility* is the characteristic indicated by the fact that "he kneeled upon his knees." Perhaps a better word is *submission.* The kneeling posture is the posture of submission.

(5) Daniel's prayer was *regular*—"three times a day," formally addressing prayer to God. Though the Bible nowhere commands any special frequency of prayer, prayer thrice daily appears to have been practiced in Bible times by other saints. David, for one, says, "I will call upon God; and the Lord will save me. Evening, and morning, and at noon, will I pray, and cry aloud, and he shall hear my voice" (Ps. 55:16-17).

(6) Daniel's prayer contained *petition.* Such is the emphasis in the words "and prayed," for it distinguished this aspect of his devotion from the giving of thanks. We are not told precisely what his requests were, but we may be sure there was fervent request for deliverance (cf. v. 11).

(7) His prayer was also marked with *thanksgiving,* for he "gave thanks before his God." This complies fully with in-

[Handwritten annotations at top: FAITH, WORSHIP, DIRECTION (PRAYER TOWARD THE HOUSE), HUMILITY, REGULAR (3 TIMES A DAY), CONTAINED PETITION, THANKSGIVING, CONSTANT]

structions for prayer in Philippians 4:6 "in every thing by prayer and supplication *with thanksgiving* let your requests be made known to God." *[THESE ELEMENTS OF PRAYER DEMON-STRATED BY DANIEL]*

(8) Finally, Daniel's prayer was *constant*. It is most important to emphasize that now under the most difficult situation, Daniel prayed "as he did aforetime." The man who has been in a habit of praying when life provides no special danger or stress is likely to find God's ear more readily "in the floods of great waters." *[TO PAGE 63 BOOK 1]*

IV. THE SUCCESS OF THE PLOT AGAINST DANIEL
(Dan. 6:11-17)

"The tender mercies of the wicked are cruel" (Prov. 12:10), and never were men either more wicked or more cruel—unless it was when the leaders of Judaism crucified the Saviour. The plot of the scheming bureaucrats worked like a charm.

A. They had "sought to find occasion against Daniel" not in his civil administration (which they complimented by acknowledging it to be flawless), but "concerning the law of his God." They could not have chosen a more vulnerable aspect of his character—vulnerable not because he would yield his principles, but precisely because he would not. So—

> Then these men assembled, and found Daniel praying and making supplication before his God (Dan. 6:11).

One meaning for the word *assembled* (as in v. 6 also) is to be in tumult, to assemble noisily and with a measure of violence. In the former case the idea is that they mobbed the king with their excited suggestion. In the second case they appeared noisily to have interrupted the old statesman at his private devotions. Both notices are intended to report their actions as unworthy of dignitaries of a great empire.

Daniel's windows had been open before; he did not close them now. He had prayed where he could be observed before; he did not cease to do so now.

B. If they had wanted the law of Daniel's God to appear to

make him a traitor to the law of the kingdom, they were eminently successful. For—

> Then they came near, and spake before the king concerning the king's decree; Hast thou not signed a decree, that every man that shall ask a petition of any God or man within thirty days, save of thee, O king, shall be cast into the den of lions? The king answered and said, the thing is true, according to the law of the Medes and the Persians, which altereth not. Then answered they and said before the king, that Daniel, which is of the children of the captivity of Judah, regardeth not thee, O king, nor the decree that thou hast signed, but maketh his petition three times a day (Dan. 6:12-13).

No mention is made of their self-serving purposes. All is made to appear as if their concern were for the king and his laws. How seldom the real reasons for actions ever come to the public eye! It was only their envy that made it necessary for them to get rid of him. Any legal cart would do to haul him off!

C. If the plotters had schemed to catch the gullible king in the technicalities of his own laws their plans worked to perfection.

> Then the king, when he heard these words, was sore displeased with himself, and set his heart on Daniel to deliver him: and he laboured till the going down of the sun to deliver him. Then these men assembled unto the king, and said unto the king, know, O king, that the law of the Medes and Persians is, that no decree nor statute which the king establisheth may be changed (Dan. 6:14-15).

The unhappy ruler found himself bound and gagged by his own law. Thus the story demonstrates the prophecy of Daniel that the kingdom to follow the Babylonian would be "a kingdom inferior" (Dan. 2:39) as regards the character of the sovereignty exercised by the rulers. Nebuchadnezzar had unlimited authority as an absolute monarch. "Whom he would he slew, and whom he would he kept alive." In the Medo-Persian, "and in each empire that followed we find imperial power more and more curtailed, and the voice of the people making itself heard with ever greater force and intensity until the days of the feet of the image, part of iron and part of brittle pottery—a union of social democracy and imperialism" (Ironside).

D. They had schemed to do away with this godly, guileless and harmless old man who had served God and man well for three-quarters of a century. In this also they appeared to be successful, for the king finding his efforts at deliverance unavailing except at the price of his own royal dignity had Daniel thrown to the lions (cf. Dan. 6:16-17). Yet that God would ultimately thwart the artful schemers, delivering His faithful servant, was suggested even by the king himself. He cried, even as Daniel was committed to the den, "Thy God whom thou servest continually [even when worship was proscribed], he will deliver thee."

V. GOD'S ANSWER TO DANIEL'S PRAYER
(Dan. 6:17-28)

"And a stone was brought, and laid upon the mouth of the den; *and the king sealed it with his own signet, and with the signet of his lords.*" (Dan. 6:17). The word for "den" is more literally "pit." Apparently the pit was covered with a lid or cover. The food was passed to the beasts through this door. This door was now closed and some plastic substance as clay or wax placed over its edge and marked with the king's own signature ring. Thus Daniel's friends would not be permitted to help him out during the night and his enemies would not be able to harm him in case God should in some manner deliver him. The parallel with the case of our Lord's body, sealed in the tomb by an official Roman seal, is most striking.

A. If Daniel prayed *for the king,* and most likely he did, then God responded initially by doing a work of grace in the king's heart. For—

> Then the king commanded, and they brought Daniel, and cast him into the den of lions. Now the king spake and said unto

Daniel, Thy God whom thou servest continually, he will deliver thee (Dan. 6:16).

Evidently the faith of Daniel had been contagious to the extent of affecting even the king. "He is able to deliver thee!" It was quite a royal confession! Any God arousing such loyalty to Himself, and such devotion as Daniel had shown is bound to be highly esteemed by observers. The kind of faith which the king saw in Daniel affected his own estimate of the God toward whom the faith was directed. What a challenge for overcoming public faith today!

After a night of fasting (a religious exercise frequently recommended in the Bible) the king rushed out early in the morning to see what had happened. He had more faith, apparently, than many Christians now have.

B. If Daniel prayed *for himself*, then verses 21-23 describe the answer. Like his friends who were not even affected by the smell of smoke, Daniel escaped from the lions' den with "no manner of hurt."

C. If Daniel prayed that the incident should *glorify his God* and benefit His kingdom, then verses 24-28 describe the threefold answer. In the first place, God's enemies (and Daniel's) were destroyed. God is not to be blamed, however, for the excessive fury which Darius directed toward the families of the plotters. Such executions, were, in fact, forbidden by Mosaic law. Darius' action was, however, in keeping with the general standards of the time. In the second place, Daniel's God was specifically confessed to be the living God. The king's Zoroastrain faith was a kind of metaphysical and ethical dualism in which on the one hand matter and evil were associated as one eternal principle; while light and good, on the other, were regarded as a second eternal principle. This was much closer to the ethical monotheism of Judah than the prevailing polytheism of antiquity. Third, God's people, especially their champion Daniel, were prospered. The ninth to the twelfth chapters of this book together with the books of Ezra and Nehemiah develop the story.

7

Daniel 7

Four Beasts, the Ancient of Days, and the Son of Man:

A Prophecy of Christ and Antichrist

I. The Historical Setting (Dan. 7:1)

II. The Details of Daniel's Visions (Dan. 7:2-14, 21-22)

III. The Method of Interpreting Daniel's Visions (Dan. 7:15-16)

IV. Details of Interpretation of Daniel's Visions (Dan. 7:17-20, 23-27)

There are two important changes in the Book of Daniel beginning with this chapter. Heretofore the material has been mainly narrative of events in Babylon wherein on two occasions Daniel interprets certain happenings as predictions of the future (Nebuchadnezzar's dream of chaps. 2 and 4). Hereafter the prophet only receives dreams, visions, and so forth. A great angel (Gabriel) appears to Daniel and provides the interpretation of his dreams and visions (see 7:16; 8:15-17; 9:20-23; 10:10-14). This is the first major change—a change of *revelatory method*. The second change is a change in Daniel's *standpoint in reporting*. Previously the author's reports have been in the third person, but after a transition at verse 1 the author takes the standpoint of first person reporter. The third person reporting ends with Daniel 7:1— "Then he [Daniel] wrote the dream." But the next verse begins: "Daniel spake and said, I saw in my vision" and so forth. "I saw" is the beginning of the first person reporting, carried on to the close of the book.

Inasmuch as most of the rest of the book is predictive prophecy, and since chapters 2 and 7 are basic to the rest of the prophecy, it is necessary to give some attention to a comparison of these chapters. Beginning with Babylon, both chapters relate how Gentile world rule would be passed on through four successive national custodies up to the coming of the "Son of Man." Then with His coming the everlasting kingdom of God is introduced. Some features of both chapters relate to events at the second coming of Christ. The New Testament clarifies some of these prophecies, but some are not treated further in the New Testament, and for that reason much of the material awaits the return of the Saviour for full exposition.

Daniel was given to see things in their inward spiritual aspect. With startling change of character the nations now appear as ferocious wild beasts—snarling and devouring one another. What realism! What likeness to the facts of past and contemporary world history! How frightening to him whose hope is "in this life" (Ps. 17:14-15).

The story ends with the final form of national dominion under the Antichrist slain like a wild beast and "committed to the burning flame."

I. THE HISTORICAL SETTING (Dan. 7:1)

> In the first year of Belshazzar king of Babylon Daniel had a dream and visions of his head upon his bed: then he wrote the dream, and told the sum of the matters (Dan. 7:1).

"The first year of Belshazzar" was likely a period of international turmoil. Likely the Persians had already begun to close in on the Babylonians by conquest and absorbtion of portions of the empire. According to best authorities this would have been 553/2 B.C., 14 years before the events of the fifth chapter of Daniel.

The distinction between "dreams" and "visions" is not always clear in the Bible. Probably the dream is the condition of having the mind active during sleep. "Visions" is intended to represent the successive scenes (or "acts," to borrow a word from the theater) of the dream. "Dream" is singular; "visions" is plural.

That Daniel "then . . . wrote the dream, and told the sum of the matters" is a very important bit of information on an obscure matter—the manner in which these Old Testament prophets received and reported the revelations God gave to them. Evidently an immediate record ("then") in written form ("he wrote") was made. This record was an abbreviated ("sum of the matters," that is, a summary) truthful report by the same man who received the revelation. The act of seeing, that is, of receiving information by dream and vision from God was "revelation." The matter received was "revelation." The record he wrote was an "inspired" one (cf. 2 Tim. 3:16).

II. THE DETAILS OF DANIEL'S VISIONS (Dan. 7:2-14, 21-22)

> Daniel spake and said, I saw in my vision by night, and, behold, the four winds of the heaven strove upon the great sea. And four great beasts came up from the sea, diverse one from another (Dan. 7:2-3).

"Upon the great sea" is not an indefinite reference but refers to the Mediterranean, thus indicating that until the consummation the center of biblical prophetic interest will remain the Mediterranean area.

Four different wild animals come before the prophet's attention. In a preliminary action "four winds of heaven brake forth" (v. 2 ASV). Usage here and elsewhere (cf. Rev. 7:1-3) indicates that the winds represent the heavenly powers by which God sets the nations of the world in motion (or commotion), and by which He controls them (cf. Jer. 51:1-3).

The word for wind (*rûach*) may be translated either wind or spirit, as the context requires. It appears to be purposefully ambiguous here, indicating that behind the symbolical winds are divinely sent spirits (Jerome thought angels).

It is to be observed that the first three of the beasts—a lion, a bear, and a leopard—were all beasts with which residents of the Near East were familiar. The fourth beast is abnormal, a destructive phenomenon like nothing ever seen in nature. This suggests the unnatural strength and ferocity of the final form of the Gentile power.

The origin of the four great beasts, "up from the sea," is interpreted as the earth in verse 17. The sea also indicates unrest (cf. Isa. 57:20). Jesus used the same figure in much the same way when He spoke of how at the time of His return there would be "upon the earth distress of nations, with perplexity; the sea and the waves roaring" (Luke 21:25). Again we should remind ourselves that the nations of earth and their governments are seldom spoken of in complimentary terms in Scripture.

I. The First Beast

> The first was like a lion, and had eagle's wings: I beheld till the wings thereof were plucked, and it was lifted up from the earth, and made stand upon the feet as a man, and a man's heart was given to it (Dan. 7:4).

The lion is a symbol of Babylon here, as also in Jeremiah 4:6-7. The "eagle's wings" speak of swiftness of movement, just as the lion pictures strength. Nebuchadnezzar's powerful conquests came mainly in the early years of his reign and were indeed accomplished swiftly. Plucking of the wings apparently speaks of an early end to expansion. The last part of the verse appears to be a direct reference to the experiences of Nebuchadnezzar recorded in chapter 4.

2. The Second Beast

> And behold another beast, a second, like to a bear, and it raised up itself on one side, and it had three ribs in the mouth of it between the teeth of it: and they said thus unto it, Arise, devour much flesh (Dan. 7:5).

The bear has always been regarded high on the scale of strength among animals. Its strength and ferocity are prominent in almost every one of the 13 references to bears in the Bible. Its ponderous bulk (some bears weigh over half a ton) fits well the massive ancient Persian armies. Duality of the Medo-Persian kingdom appears to be indicated by the fact that the two sides of the bear are indicated. Compare the two arms, two breasts, and so on, of the image of chapter 2.

3. The Third Beast

> After this I beheld, and lo another, like a leopard, which had upon the back of it four wings of a fowl; the beast had also four heads; and dominion was given to it (Dan. 7:6).

The leopard stands, like the belly and thighs of Nebuchadnezzar's dream-image, for the so-called Grecian kingdom of Alexander the Great and his successors.

The sinewy, lithe, swift leopard aptly stands both for Alexander and for his kingdom. If Nebuchadnezzar moved with two wings, then Alexander moved with four. Alexander's kingdom, unlike either the Persian or the Babylonian, soon became subdivided, as is indicated by the four heads.

Rulership passed to Babylon from Nineveh (Assyria) in 612 B.C.; from Babylon to Medo-Persia in about 539 B.C. (as described in chap. 5), from the Medo-Persians to Alexander late in the fourth century B.C. in a series of engagements in Asia Minor, Syria, and Mesopotamia.

Alexander's father, Philip, by warfare united Greece in 338 B.C. Upon his death two years later, his son succeeded him. During the 13 years of his reign (336-323 B.C.) Alexander performed some of the greatest feats of military valor known to man before or since.

The four heads of the leopard appear to stand for the fourfold division of his empire shortly after his death. "Dominion" is said to have been "given unto" this monstrous leopard and nothing could be closer to the exact truth. Alexander could conquer about anything except himself—he died of dissipation (at least many historians think so) at Babylon, in the thirty-second year of his age, 323 B.C.

4. The Fourth Beast

> After this I saw in the night visions, and behold a fourth beast, dreadful and terrible, and strong exceedingly; and it had great iron teeth: it devoured and brake in pieces, and stamped the residue with the feet of it: and it was diverse from all the beasts that were before it; and it had ten horns. I considered the horns, and, behold, there came up among them another little horn, before whom there were three of the first plucked up by the roots: and, behold, in this horn were eyes like the eyes of man, and a mouth speaking great things (Dan. 7:7-8).

The revealing angel picks out this beast, its 10 horns and the little horn among them for special explanatory treatment later in chapter 7, thus cursory attention only is necessary here. Just as in the dream-image of chapter 4, the *fourth stage* of world dominion is the Roman. Inasmuch as this stage of dominion is presented as prevailing until the destruction of Antichrist and the establishment of the eternal kingdom of Christ, it must be regarded as continuing in some sense today, and as operating in a very lively way at the very consummation of the present age. Observe that a *tenfold division* of this kingdom, as was suggested by Daniel chapter 2, and as verified by Revelation 17:3 and following, is indicated here by 10 horns. The little horn is identified with the Antichrist of the last days later in the chapter.

5. The Ancient of Days and the Son of Man

> I beheld till the thrones were cast down, and the Ancient of days did sit, whose garment was white as snow, and the hair of his head like the pure wool: his throne was like the fiery flame, and his wheels as burning fire. A fiery stream issued and came forth from before him: thousand thousands ministered unto him, ten thousands times ten thousand stood before him: the judgment was set, and the books were opened (Dan. 7:9-10).

"Till the thrones were cast down" should be rendered "till thrones were set in position." With this small explanation a truly magnificent scene flashes up before us. This is the awful Majesty, the Godhead, sitting to judge and bring to an end the course of human government in the hands of wicked men. The several thrones are for the Almighty and for his "four and twenty elders" (Rev. 4:2-4). "Ancient of days"— the very aged one—is none other than "the high and lofty One that inhabiteth eternity, whose name is Holy" (Isa. 57:15). The whiteness of His hair suggests holiness. The fire of His throne and the "river of fire" coming from His throne suggest judgment. The wheels remind the Bible-versed reader of the magnificent vision of the Godhead in Ezekiel's earliest chapters. The thousand thousands and the ten thousands times ten thousand standing at reverent attention show with what respect God is held in heaven, and yet to be had on earth.

> I beheld then because of the voice of the great words which the horn spake: I beheld even till the beast was slain, and his body destroyed, and given to the burning flame. As concerning the rest of the beasts, they had their dominion taken away: yet their lives were prolonged for a season and time (Dan. 7:11-12).

What is to become of the Antichrist and his supporters? A full description is provided the reader in the nineteenth chapter of Revelation.

"The rest of the beasts" are the first three of the series: the winged lion, the bear, and the four-winged, four-headed leopard. That "their lives were prolonged" and so forth, means only that each lived out its time in world dominion in accordance with the plan of God. It does not mean that they survive the fourth kingdom in any sense.

> I saw in the night visions, and, behold, one like the Son of man came with the clouds of heaven, and came to the Ancient of days, and they brought him near before him. And there was given him dominion, and glory, and a kingdom, that all people, nations, and languages, should serve him: his kingdom is an everlasting dominion, which shall not pass away, and his kingdom that which shall not be destroyed (Dan. 7:13-14).

These two verses constitute one of the most important links in the Bible between the Old Testament and the New. Practically everything in these verses the New Testament claims for the one known therein as Jesus of Nazareth. Jesus' favorite name for Himself was "the Son of man." The Aramaic of Daniel 7:13, to be sure, may be read simply "one like a son of man," that is, a human being. But the fact remains that Jesus applied it to Himself, apparently in the special sense of the *one representative man*.

Paul calls Jesus "the last Adam" and pointedly connects the phrase with heavenly origin (cf. 1 Cor. 15:45-47). In this context the phrase implies, if not deity, then close connection with deity. His coming "with the clouds of heaven" has similar connections. Jesus describes His second advent as "the Son of man coming in the clouds of heaven with power and great glory" (Matt. 24:30). Those clouds were seen at His ascension (cf. Acts 1:9) and will be seen again when He returns (cf. Acts 1:11; 1 Thess. 4:17; Rev. 1:7).

It should be clear to men today that the final manifestation of the kingdom has not yet arrived. The details of this passage cannot be applied to conditions or events of the present age. The arrogant beasts are still running things and the loudmouthed, blaspheming "little horn" has not even yet appeared, even though he has had many similar predecessors.

The student should now read the concluding portion of the visions before considering other matters.

6. The War of the "Little Horn" with the "Saints"

I beheld, and the same horn made war with the saints, and prevailed against them; until the Ancient of days came, and judgment was given to the saints of the most High; and the time came that the saints possessed the kingdom (Dan. 7:21-22).

A practical matter and a doctrinal matter are each suggested. (1.) The right kind of people are at last to come into their kingdom. Those known as "saints," which really means "holy people," are they whom God has chosen to be in charge at last.

(2.) The victory of might over right is only temporary. God is still on His throne.

Specifically and doctrinally considered, however, this passage is affirming that God's ancient holy people, the Hebrews, scattered and oppressed at the time of the prophecy, are yet to receive their kingdom on earth as promised to a whole succession of prophets from Abraham to the Apostle Paul. Daniel 8:24 is clear that the "holy people" are the Jews.

It is true, of course, that the New Testament many times affirms that Christian believers of this age already share in a present kingdom of God (cf. Col. 1:13) and shall yet reign with Christ in a future kingdom (Rev. 2:25-27). It is also true that our Lord entered upon a heavenly reign when He sat down at the right hand of the majesty on high. We do affirm, however, that such does not appear to be what Daniel is talking about.

III. THE METHOD OF INTERPRETING DANIEL'S VISIONS (Dan. 7:15-16)

I Daniel was grieved in my spirit in the midst of my body, and the visions of my head troubled me. I came near unto one of them that stood by, and asked him the truth of all this. So he told me, and made me know the interpretation of the things (Dan. 7:15-16).

Troubled to know what was going on in his head he approached one of the visionary angels to ask him the meaning of it all. Whereupon this visionary angel turns out to be not a vision at all, but a real angel, Gabriel the archangel (cf. 8:16; 9:21).

IV. DETAILS OF INTERPRETATION OF DANIEL'S VISIONS (Dan. 7:17-20; 23-27)

1. The Lesser Emphasis: the four beasts in relation to God's kingdom.

> These great beasts, which are four, are four kings, which shall arise out of the earth. But the saints of the most High shall take the kingdom, and possess the kingdom for ever, even for ever and ever (Dan. 7:17-18).

The lines of interpretation of the passage, as paralleling the four stages of Gentile dominion, succeeded by Christ's kingdom as predicted (chap. 2), I have already given. There is, however, another quite respectable evangelical view of the four beasts. Taking their cue from the angel's statement that these beasts are "four kings, which *shall* arise," and observing the Babylonian kingdom was already in the position of world dominion, a minority of interpreters insists that all four kingdoms are "eschatological," that is, related to the final form of dominion just before the return of the Lord. Holding that the visions do not go again over the ground of the dream-image prophecy of chapter 2, they assert that this chapter relates to how the kingdom at the time of the "feet and toes" of the image will develop. The arguments furnished by supporters (chiefly Sir Robert Anderson and G. H. Lang) are very convincing.

2. The Greater Emphasis: the final form of the fourth beast in relation to the kingdom of God.

> Then I would know the truth of the fourth beast, which was diverse from all the others, exceeding dreadful, whose teeth were of iron, and his nails of brass; which devoured and brake in pieces, and stamped the residue with his feet.... Thus he said, The fourth beast shall be the fourth kingdom upon the earth, which shall be diverse from all kingdoms, and shall devour the

whole earth, and shall tread it down, and break it in pieces (Dan. 7:19, 23).

This corresponds with the statements in chapter 2 concerning this fourth kingdom that as iron it would "break in pieces and subdue" (Dan. 2:40). It is evidently that system of world government which was introduced by Rome in the last two centuries before the Christian era, and became supreme at the conquest of Egypt by Caesar in the middle of the first century B.C. The system prevails today in what is called western civilization and may be expected to be in vigorous condition at the very end of our age.

Without attempting to predict precisely what political or geographical shape it will assume, there are many reasons for believing some "Romish" form of empire will prevail till Jesus comes again. (1) Chapter 2 teaches that the fourth of these kingdoms will be in existence until violently destroyed by Christ at His coming. This has not yet occurred. (2) The tenfold form of the kingdom is the form of the kingdom at its destruction (vv. 7-8, 24). Such a form of world dominion does not seem yet to have taken place in history. (3) The similarity of this fourth beast to the beast of Revelation 13:1-2 and 17:3-8 suggests identity. John's prophecy is of a kingdom to be destroyed by Christ at His second advent. John's beast, like Daniel's, comes out of the sea (Rev. 13:1), both have 10 horns (Rev. 13:1), both are blasphemous (Rev. 13:5), each is in connection with a leopard, a bear, and a lion (Rev. 13:2). John looking backward on the three saw them in reverse order from Daniel's.

> And of the ten horns that were in his head, and of the other which came up, and before whom three fell; even of that horn that had eyes, and a mouth that spake very great things, whose look was more stout than his fellows.... And the ten horns out of this kingdom are ten kings that shall arise: and another shall rise after them; and he shall be diverse from the first, and he shall subdue three kings (Dan. 7:20, 24).

The verses are saying that 10 horns are 10 kings who shall

rise in the final state of the fourth kingdom. They correspond to the 10-toed stage of the image that shall reign contemporaneously in the end-time as is prophesied likewise in Revelation 17:12 and following.

The little horn is the coming Antichrist, and men of about every kind of persuasion concerning "last things" agree that he is some kind of consummate antichrist. Let us read the material about him here and then summarize the information given about this one called by Paul the "man of sin," "the son of perdition" (2 Thess. 2:3), and "that Wicked [one]" (2 Thess. 2:8).

> And the ten horns out of this kingdom are ten kings that shall arise: and another shall rise after them; and he shall be diverse from the first, and he shall subdue three kings. And he shall speak great words against the most High, and shall wear out the saints of the most High, and think to change times and laws: and they shall be given into his hand until a time and times and the dividing of time (Dan. 7:24-25).

(1) The Antichrist shall arise after the tenfold form of the final world dominion has developed. The "little horn" was observed by Daniel after he had "considered" the 10 horns awhile (v. 8), and he is said to come "after them" (v. 24). He will evidently not create a confederacy of 10 kings but will absorb such a confederacy.

(2) He is only "another ... horn"—just another king. Even though Satan may energize him, he is mortal and will die. These matters are made clear in the New Testament (Rev. 13:2; 2 Thess. 2:8-9).

(3) He begins as a *"little* horn." We may expect him to be obscure at first, not bursting upon the world with a glare of satanic splendor, but winning his way gradually.

(4) He will begin his march to world dominion by first subduing three other kings of the tenfold alliance, for "there came up among them another little horn, before whom there were three of the first horns plucked up by the roots" (v. 8). In verse 24 Gabriel adds that "he shall subdue three kings."

This is to be the beginning of world conquest.

(5) Though he is only "another" horn, yet there will be something unique about him, for "he shall be diverse from the first"—that is, the 10 kings. He will indeed have a different form of government. His will be the most absolute dictatorship the world has known. He shall enforce worship of himself (cf. Rev. 13:15; 2 Thess. 2:4) and shall impose sanctions successfully that have only been *tried* before. He shall cause "all, both small and great, rich and poor, free and bond, to receive a mark in their right hand, or in their foreheads: and that no man might buy or sell, save he that had the mark, or the name of the beast, or the number of his name" (Rev. 13:16-17). He will also be "diverse" personally. Some of the strangest sounding statements in the Bible are about him, almost all of them cryptic remarks, still not fully understood. His "coming is after the working of Satan with all power and signs and lying wonders, and with deceivableness" (2 Thess. 2:9-10, cf. Rev. 13:13-14).

(6) Antichrist is to be unusually intelligent, or perhaps the meaning is "commanding personality." This is suggested not only by the many statements about his amazing career, but also by the information that the horn will have "eyes like the eyes of man" (v. 8), for human eyes can tell a lot about the intelligence of their human possessors.

(7) He will also be an orator of ability—he will have "a mouth speaking great things" (v. 8). He will doubtless be a self-exalted braggart—suggested by translating "a mouth speaking big things." But probably the vision intends to suggest that he will have persuasive ability.

(8) His personal appearance will correspond with his position—he will "look the part" as they say in the theater, for Daniel observed that "his look was more stout than his fellows" (v. 20). We might better translate it as "his appearance more impressive than that of his contemporaries." This man, we may be sure, will be dressed for his part and will have a well-coached and staged entrance upon the platform of world affairs.

(9) He will be a blasphemer, speaking "great words against the most High" (v. 25). John writes, "speaking great things and blasphemies . . . against God, to blaspheme his name, and his tabernacle, and them that dwell in heaven" (Rev. 13:5-6). Neither Daniel nor John were given to foresee the general victory of anti-supernatural attitudes in the world today. However, it seems probably that these blasphemies will be some consummate form of the secularistic, naturalistic philosophy steadily gaining ground in our day.

(10) Antichrist will seek to establish his kingdom and himself as the beginning of a new epoch: he shall "think to change times and laws" (v. 25). He will doubtless do this with the zeal of secular moralist temper. One can safely imagine that even dating a letter as such and such a year A.D., the year of our Lord, will be personally offensive to this "man of sin." Like the French revolutionists he may seek to abolish the traditional week and the year of 12 months. Marriage and other common civil laws will likely come in for attack.

In verse 25 comes a most important transitional statement—the statement that changes the subject matter of Daniel as well as the language of his book. This beast "shall wear out the saints [the holy people] of the most High." God's people, the holy people of Israel, become now the subject of the book onward to the end, and accordingly at the end of this vision the language shifts from Aramaic back to Hebrew, left off at Daniel 2:4.

(11) The period during which Antichrist shall have unrestricted power is limited to a brief period. What appears to be best understood as three and one-half years (v. 25) is elaborated by John to be 42 months (cf. Rev. 13:5, 11:2). Daniel later refers to the same as a period of one-half a "week [seven]" (Dan. 9:27; see also Dan. 12:7, 11-12). This limited period of time is a matter of great interest and of elaborate treatment in the Bible. Later chapters of Daniel will provide opportunity to study it further.

> But the judgment shall sit, and they shall take away his dominion, to consume and to destroy it unto the end. And the

kingdom and dominion, and the greatness of the kingdom under the whole heaven, shall be given to the people of the saints of the most High, whose kingdom is an everlasting kingdom, and all dominions shall serve and obey him (Dan. 7:26-27).

Two words herein call for some explanation: "kingdom and dominion." "Kingdom" is derived from the word for king, and is pronounced *malkûth*. It may refer either to rulership, the act of ruling; to the right of rulership or sovereignty; or to the realms, that is, the sphere, in which rule is exercised. Sometimes one, sometimes another of these ideas is paramount. "Dominion" is *sholtan*, related to the Arabic word, *sultan*, used of rulers in Islamic countries. It is a synonym with almost exactly the same range of meanings.

Antichrist shall come to his end. He whose name is "The Word of God" shall destroy this loathsome beast with the "breath of his lips." There shall follow a Millennium during which these poor persecuted people of God, the Hebrews, shall inherit their promise of peace in possession of their ancient land of Canaan (see Isa. 2:1-5; Jer. 31:22-40). In their resurrection bodies the saints of the Church Age shall join with them to "reign with him [our Lord Jesus] a thousand years" (see Rev. 20:1-6). This thousand-year period is only an initial stage of this coming kingdom, for God's kingdom is "that which shall not be destroyed" and shall be possessed by his saints "for ever, even for ever and ever" (Dan. 7:14, 18, cf. 2:44).

Since a particular view, heretofore referred to as *premillennialism,* has been assumed in this exposition, I feel that I have a duty to mention competing views and to present some of the main reasons why I adopt this view which I am recommending to my readers. Most *postmillennialists,* who expect the Saviour to return after a period when Christianity shall have prevailed over all the earth for 1,000 years (that is, for the Millennium), feel that the "little horn" of Antichrist, is either the Pope or the Roman Church. The victory of Christ's kingdom is thought to be accomplished gradually during the present age. Most contemporary *amillennialists* feel that the

Millennium of Revelation 20 is the present reign of the deceased saints in heaven with Christ, and that at the end of this age they will come with Christ to destroy the beast, whom they, with us, feel to be a real Gentile king. Their view of the course of the present age, when good and evil grow together, is similar to premillennialism. There are at least five reasons, all drawn from the context of this chapter, why I (as most premillenarians) feel these competing views should be rejected in favor of the one adopted herein.

A. The kingdom of Messiah is clearly *to follow* the appearance of Antichrist, and his destruction, events still future. These events are in near connection with Christ's return. This is the strongest reason, and appears to make both amillennialism and postmillennialism impossible.

B. The prophecy requires that the visible kingdom of Christ, as considered in Daniel, chapter 7, follow the kingdoms of the Gentiles—they are not to be at any period contemporary. This would eliminate the amillennial scheme.

C. The visible kingdom of "the most High" succeeds a final form of the fourth Gentile dominion (a 10-fold one) which has not yet appeared. John, apparently, predicted that final form of Gentile dominion as still future in his own day. And as far as we know it has not yet appeared today. The visible kingdom of Christ must, therefore, still be future.

D. The visible kingdom of Messiah to be established, as predicted in the chapter, appears to take over the realms of the earlier kingdoms, and to be, as many other predictions specify, one of outward power and glory. The present reign of Christ in the hearts of believers or in heaven hardly meets these specifications. Christ's realm on earth, at the present time, appears to be one where His spiritual subjects continue to suffer and to bear crosses.

E. In some special sense the kingdom of Messiah is going to be Jewish, as the language of this chapter requires. This is not true of any present kingdom of Christ on earth, except that the Saviour Himself, and the original founders of the Church (apostles) were Jewish.

8

Daniel 8

A Ram, a Goat, and a Little Horn:

Prophecy of Israel in Conflict with the Old Testament Antichrist

I. The Historical Introduction (Dan. 8:1)

II. The Visions (Dan. 8:2-14)

III. The Interpretation (Dan. 8:15-26)

IV. The Historical Conclusion (Dan. 8:27)

One who becomes acquainted with the whole Bible will discover a great deal of repetition therein. The entire history of the Old Testament is covered twice in the Old Testament: once in Genesis through 2 Kings, a second time in the books of Chronicles. The life of Christ is presented four times in the four Gospels. The prophets of the Old Testament repeat one another in their predictions, too. Isaiah, Jeremiah, and Ezekiel present similar oracles against several of the nations round about them, and the downfall of Assyria is predicted many times in Isaiah alone.

Yet none of the repetitions is an *identical* repetition. Each presentation is from a different point of view; new details are added; new emphases are made. Those who have carefully read the four Gospels are made well aware of this.

Chapter 8 of Daniel is a third prophetic discussion of two of the four great kingdoms of the Gentiles: the second (Persian) and the third (Greek). The breasts and arms of the image prophecy of chapter 4, the second beast (a bear) of chapter 7, and now the two-horned ram of chapter 8 are all figures of the kingdom of the Medes and Persians. The belly and thighs of the image, the four-headed leopard of chapter 7, and the one-horned buck goat of the present study are figures of the coming kingdom of Greece, under Alexander.

I. THE HISTORICAL INTRODUCTION (Dan. 8:1)

In the third year of the reign of king Belshazzar a vision appeared unto me, even unto me Daniel, after that which appeared unto me at the first (Dan. 8:1).

The third year of Belshazzar, according to evidences now available, would likely have been about 551 B.C. A vision had come to Daniel two years earlier, the vision of the four beast and the Ancient of Days (cf. 7:1). Considering the fact that this would have been some years before the sacrilegious feast of Belshazzar and the end of the Babylonian kingdom (539 B.C.), it may account for Daniel's eclipse as a royal adviser during Belshazzar's reign.

II. THE VISIONS (Dan. 8:2-14)

1. The Scene of Daniel's Visions

> And I saw in a vision; and it came to pass, when I saw, that I was at Shushan in the palace, which is in the province of Elam; and I saw in a vision, and I was by the river of Ulai (Dan. 8:2).

There has been discussion as to whether Daniel was in Shushan in vision, transported there in spirit only, or if he was literally there on the business of the king (cf. v. 27) and while there had the vision. As far as Daniel's experience is concerned, the language of verse 2 seems clearly to state that it was not in the flesh but only in the vision he was in Shushan.

Elam at various times was an independent nation. At the time of the prophecy it was subject to Babylon. At the time of the Persian Empire, predicted by the vision, it was a province of the empire, and its capital city, Shushan, usually spelled Susa, was one of several capitals of the empire. Susa was not an important place in the third year of Belshazzar, but this city, only 250 miles due east of Babylon, became the Persian capital nearest to Babylon in a few short years. This appears to be why the scene of the vision is that place.

"The palace," then would not have been a Babylonian structure but a Persian one, perhaps not yet in literal existence at the time Daniel saw it.

"The palace"—granting that Daniel has reference to the great palace which the Persian kings were to build—was truly magnificent. Xerxes, the Ahasuerus of Esther (486-465 B.C.), was its builder. There Esther would have lived and most of the events of the Book of Esther took place at this palace in Shushan.

One further geographical notice, "by the river of Ulai," calls for some attention. Though this river is not mentioned in Esther, it is mentioned in the Assyrian inscriptions relating to Susa. The Greeks report that Alexander sailed down this stream to the Persian Gulf. For many years geographers wondered how Alexander could have done this, for Ulai was usually identified with a canal in the region. About a century ago it was discovered that a now extinct branch of a large river flowed near Shushan. It was likely on this river branch that Daniel was situated in his vision.

2. The Vision of a Ram

> Then I lifted up mine eyes, and saw, and, behold, there stood before the river a ram which had two horns: and the two horns were high; but one was higher than the other, and the higher came up last (Dan. 8:3).

The Hebrew word for ram (*ayil*) is derived from a verb which means to be in front. In both domestic and wild state a flock of sheep moves with the strongest male in front. So the word was a natural term for human leaders and kings.

As in chapter 7 the horns stand both for kings and kingdoms. Here the duality of the Medo-Persian dominion is indicated by the two horns. Their union is indicated by the ram itself. The fact that the older power, the Median, had been superseded by the younger, the Persian, is indicated by the fact that though the shorter horn, it had appeared earlier than the other.

Herodotus reports tales about Cyrus to the effect that he was of mixed Median and Persian ancestry. He includes a fascinating story about Cyrus being reared in Persia *incognito*. Whatever his manner of origin, it was under Cyrus' leadership that the Persians became masters of the Medes in the coalition.

> And I saw the ram pushing westward, and northward, and southward; so that no beasts might stand before him, neither was there any that could deliver out of his hand; but did according to his will, and became great (Dan. 8:4).

Northward. The Hebrew word "northward" (Dan. 8:4) simply means "the unknown." Perhaps the cold winds and fierce peoples who seemed always to come from that way inspired a fear of northern parts, then as now.

Cyrus and his son Cambyses who succeeded him were irresistible. No kingdom could stand against them. Indeed they did what they willed, and that quite despotically. Their empire became the richest of all empires of antiquity. The ram did "become great."

3. The Vision of the He Goat

> And as I was considering, behold, an he goat came from the west on the face of the whole earth, and touched not the ground: and the goat had a notable horn between his eyes (Dan. 8:5).

The Hebrew words for directions were all graphic. That for the west, though frequently simply "the sea" (as in v. 4) from the fact that the Mediterranean Sea was the western border of Palestine, is here $m\overset{v}{a}\overset{v}{a}r\bar{a}bh$, a very strange word, indeed. It is derived from the word $\overset{,}{e}rebh$ for evening which was in turn from a verb meaning to enter. Since the sun enters night in the west the idea of "entering-of-the-sun" is the meaning of this word for west.

By now everyone will have observed that both the animals of this chapter are *common domestic animals.* They are far different from the voracious bear, standing for Persia, and the fierce swift leopard for Greece of chapter 7. The change is likely due to the fact that in chapter 7 the nations are chiefly represented in their relations one to another. In that they were ravenous, seeking to devour one another. Here their relationship to and treatment of Israel is chiefly in view. And though firm lord and in secure control of Israel, Cyrus and his successors were kind to the Jews.

The typical use of sheep and goats in general, and of the males of the two species in particular, is interesting. The buck of the goats was thought of as being superior in strength to the ram. So here is confirmation of the meaning of the image vision of chapter 2 and the four-beast vision of chapter 7. While the kingdoms may decrease in worth and the kings base their rule on a poorer grade of sovereignty, the kingdoms are nevertheless stronger as they progress toward their destruction at the coming of Messiah's kingdom.

Now, focusing attention on the he goat: observe that he comes "from the west." Macedonia was across the Hellaspont, the narrow space of water separating Asia from Europe. When Alexander took his armies across that stretch of water, he changed the course of history for the following two and one-half millenniums, and perhaps forever. At that time, the center of the world dominion shifted from the Orient to the Occident. The East had been supreme before—Egypt, Assyria, Babylon, Medes and Persians were all of the East. Alexander was of the West. Never again did the balance of world power shift to the East. The advancing civilization of the world from that day to this has been the civilization of the West.

The goat came "on the face of the whole earth," that is, he swept all before him, and since he "touched not the ground" it is understood that he came most swiftly. The most notable feature of the goat is his single horn, representing as we are later told, the first great king, Alexander.

Alexander's army, superbly organized and equipped by his father Philip, employed what was known as the *phalanx*—infantry formed in close and deep ranks with shields joined together and spears overlapping. The Persian forces simply were carved in pieces. The Greeks cut them up like a piece of pie.

All of Asia Minor was Alexander's in a few months. The next spring he passed through the Taurus Mountains in southern Asia Minor, at the Cilician Gates, and shortly thereafter engaged the Persian armies at Issus near Antioch. This time Darius arrived in great style with a massive army, and with his family and court in attendance, intending to recover lost prestige. His huge army of 600,000 was decisively defeated—the king's mother, queen, and children being captured. Darius himself escaped.

But Alexander was taking "all the earth" as he came, so he turned southward, intending to take all of Syria and Egypt before turning eastward again. The capture of Tyre detained him seven months. It was two years before he gave further attention to Darius.

4. The Victory of the He Goat over the Ram

And I saw him come close unto the ram, and he was moved with choler against him, and smote the ram, and brake his two horns: and there was no power in the ram to stand before him, but he cast him down to the ground, and stamped upon him: and there was none that could deliver the ram out of his hand (Dan. 8:7).

After the conquest of Egypt by Alexander, the he goat did, indeed, "come close unto the ram." Near the ancient city of Nineveh, on the plain of Arbela, the Macedonians met Darius and his immense army. This was the third meeting of the Greeks with the Persian army of Darius, the second, with the emperor himself in command. The army of Darius was hopelessly defeated and he himself was assassinated on the field by Bessus, satrap of Bactria. Alexander, with characteristic impulsive generosity, avenged Darius of his murderer and had him buried with regal pomp. He moved on and after taking Susa, where he seized enormous wealth in gold, "moved with choler [anger]" against the ancient Persian capital of Persepolis (Persian, *Parsa*) he utterly destroyed the city and the neighboring Ekbatana which was likewise burned.

5. The Vision of Final Growth and Division of the "Notable" Horn's Dominion

Therefore the he goat waxed very great: and when he was strong, the great horn was broken; and for it came up four notable ones toward the four winds of heaven (Dan. 8:8).

After the destruction of the last Persian resistance (331 B.C.) Alexander continued his conquests eastward, conquering the territories we now know as Iran, Afghanistan, Pakistan, and India, marrying a captive Bactrian princess, Roxana, along the way. It was at Babylon, in the thirteenth year of his reign and in the thirty-third year of his life (323 B.C.), the little genius died, the victim of fever and alcohol (say some historians). Thus it was that "the great horn was broken."

Though he had intended that his child by Roxana should have his throne, it was not to be. Instead, after about 20 years of international brawling and quarreling among Alexander's leading supporters, his lands were divided among "four notable ones," just as Daniel had said.

Only two of the four new Grecian kingdoms are of special interest here: that of Egypt and adjacent lands under Ptolemy, and that of Syria and environs, under Seleucus. These two kings and their successors become the kings of the South and of the North, respectively, in Daniel. Out of the king of the North came the "little horn," which now occupies the center of the prophet's interest.

6. The Vision of the "Little Horn" and His Conflict with Israel

This is the heart of the prophecy, for it prepared the people of Israel with knowledge of some of the very details of coming sufferings in the second century before Christ.

> And out of one of them came forth a little horn, which waxed exceeding great, toward the south, and toward the east, and toward the pleasant land (Dan. 8:9).

Commentators of all shades of opinion generally agree on the identity of this new king. He is Antiochus IV, called *Epiphanes* (Magnificent), a king in the line of Seleucus, reigning in Syria about 175-163 B.C. The student should be very careful to distinguish this little horn out of the *third* or Grecian kingdom from the little horn of chapter 7, which is out of the *fourth*, or "Roman," kingdom. Although it may be true, as we shall see, that Antiochus was a type of the final Antichrist symbolized by the little horn of chapter 7, the two are not identical.

This verse simply indicates that Antiochus would try to expand his holdings toward the south (Egypt) and toward the east (Mesopotamia, and so forth). It also indicates that he would have interests in Palestine. Palestine is indicated as "the pleasant land." The word "land" is not in the Hebrew, and the word "pleasant" might better be "beautiful" or "glorious." This was the "land flowing with milk and honey" and of Jerusalem, "beautiful for situation, the joy of the whole earth" (Ps. 48:2). Only a Jew could have written this chapter. It truly reflects the "home-town" point of view.

> And it waxed great, even to the host of heaven; and it cast down some of the host and of the stars to the ground, and stamped upon them (Dan. 8:10).

This verse seems to be a prediction of Antiochus' attack upon the people of God in Judah, and especially upon the high priest and other legal priests.

> Yea, he magnified himself even to the prince of the host, and by him the daily sacrifice was taken away, and the place of his sanctuary was cast down (Dan. 8:11).

Whether the "prince of the host" be God or the high priest, the meaning is clear. Antiochus was to attack the center of Jewish worship, and interrupt the ritual worship centered there. The full story is told in 1 Maccabees 1:20-50. Since many of the readers of this treatment will not have access to the Apocrypha, the significant portions are here excerpted.

According to this report Antiochus "entered the sanctuary, and took away the golden altar, and the candlestick, and all the vessels thereof; and the table of shew-bread, the pouring vessels... and stripped the temple of the ornaments of gold." Two years later he again "smote it very sore, and destroyed much people of Israel, and when he had taken the spoils of the city he set it on fire, and pulled down the walls thereof on every side." In addition to this "Her [Jerusalem's] sanctuary was laid waste like a wilderness, her feasts were turned into mourning, her Sabbaths into reproach, her honour into contempt." He outlawed all worship of Jehovah in the city and polluted and defiled everything in connection with the sanctuary. "For the king had sent letters by messengers unto Jerusalem and the cities of Judah, that they should follow the strange laws of the land [that is, new laws commanding worship of Greek gods and goddesses and vile pagan rites], and forbid burnt-offerings, and sacrifices, and drink-offerings in the temple; and that they should profane the Sabbaths and festival days; and pollute the sanctuary and holy people; set up altars, and groves, and chapels of idols, and sacrifice swine's flesh, and unclean beasts; that they should also leave their children uncircumcized, and make their souls abominable with all manner of uncleanness and profanation; to the end they might forget the laws and change the ordinances."

> And an host was given him against the daily sacrifice by reason of transgression, and it cast down the truth to the ground; and it practiced, and prospered (Dan. 8:12).

This means that because of the sins of the Jews in Palestine (they who returned under Zerubbabel, Ezra, Nehemiah, and so forth, and became apostate), God allowed this sad thing to happen.

> Then I heard one saint speaking, and another saint said unto that certain saint which spake, How long shall be the vision concerning the daily sacrifice, and the transgression of desolation, to give both the sanctuary and the host to be trodden under foot? And he said unto me, Unto two thousand and three hundred days; then shall the sanctuary be cleaned (Dan. 8:13-14).

Change the word "saint" to "holy one" (that is, an angel) and the words "two thousand and three hundred days" to "two thousand and three hundred *evening-mornings.*" The "evening-mornings" were of course the morning and evening burnt-offerings prescribed in Leviticus. This would be only 1,150 days, somewhat over three years. It is true that the temple was desolate for a period about that long after Antiochus desolated it and until the Maccabeean forces restored the worship.

III. THE INTERPRETATION (Dan. 8:15-26)

A. Gabriel, the revealing angel (Dan. 8:15-16). This is the first time in Scripture that the name of an angel is given—

Gabriel. The name means "hero of God." Mentioned also at Daniel 9:21 as well as Luke 1:19, 26. In Daniel 10:13 he is associated with Michael.

B. The effect of the vision on Daniel (Dan. 8:17-18). That a man of such well-recognized holiness as Daniel should be "afraid" and fall upon his face at the approach of the angel demonstrates something of the moral gulf which separates God and His holy angels from mere mortals. Imagine with what immense relief Daniel heard Gabriel's reassuring words and felt his touch.

Incidentally, this passage demonstrates some basic similarity between the normal visible form of angels and the form of men.

C. The scope of the prophecy (Dan. 8:19). By "scope" I have in mind the times during which the predictions would be fulfilled. It would seem obvious from the standpoint of today that all was fulfilled during the times of the ancient Persians and Greeks. But is this strictly true? In verse 19 Gabriel says, "I will make thee know what shall be in the last end of the *indignation:* for at the time appointed *the end* shall be." In chapter 11 (v. 36) "the indignation" is a period of divine wrath at the close of this present age. And while "the end" could be the end of the dominion of Antiochus or of the trials connected with him, yet it also frequently has eschatological connections. This is the first suggestion that perhaps the vision relates not only to Antiochus and persecutions of Jews in ancient times, but also to something in the "last days." If so, this is not an unusual feature of prophecy, which quite frequently contains elements of the near future together with the more remote future in a comprehensive grasp.

D. Medo-Persia, Greece, Alexander and his successors (Dan. 8:20-22). The interpretation of these verses has already been presented in connection with the earlier verses on the same subjects.

E. "The king of fierce countenance" (Dan. 8:23-26). These words interpret the vision of the little horn with the addition of several details not furnished in the vision. It is obviously the main point of the revelation.

Note the phrase "the mighty and the holy people." There is a word for "mighty" or "many" or "much" which is used of Israel frequently. That word is used in verse 25. Here the word is a different Hebrew word. One commentator asserts that "mighty" refers to mighty men in general, especially heathen rulers. The "holy people" are as usual, the Jewish people. This then is a cryptic way of saying this wicked king shall destroy both Gentiles and Jews.

This "king of fierce countenance" will come in "the latter time of their kingdom," that is, of the Grecian kingdom, when Jewish "transgressors" have come to the full. This king shall understand "dark sentences"—riddles, conundrums, difficult matters. He shall attack successfully the holy people, gaining power over them by trickery and diplomacy. But when he stands up against the Prince of princes he shall be destroyed by divine judgment.

The breaking of a man "without hand" here (v. 25) designates a divine visitation of judgment. This really happened to Antiochus. He left his capital in Syria for Persia, hoping to gain booty and tribute there, and committed his wars in Palestine to a certain Lysias. Repulsed in the East, Antiochus was forced to retire to Babylon. At the same time Lysias and his armies were driven out of Judah. This feat was accomplished by the army of the Maccabees which also retrieved not only much of their own stolen goods but that of other lands. Says the Maccabeean writer: "Now when the king heard these words, he was astonished and sore moved: whereupon he laid him down upon his bed, and fell sick for grief, because it had not befallen him that he looked for. And there he continued many days: for his grief was ever more and more." Then calling his friends to tell them he knew he was to die, he said, "I remember the evils that I did at Jerusalem ... I perceive therefore for this cause ... I perish.... So king Antiochus died" (1 Maccabees 8:8-16).

Now there are commentators who think that this prophecy was entirely fulfilled in Antiochus. There are others who feel that Antiochus only partially fulfills it. The latter group points out the several expressions which are difficult to apply to Antiochus. He was not noted as a particularly wise man in handling the "dark sentences." True he was a tricky diplomat, but good diplomacy is another matter. That his mighty power would be "not by his own power" sounds strangely like the declaration of John concerning the great beast of the end-time (cf. Rev. 13:2). It is not evidently applicable to Antiochus.

The "Prince of princes" sounds like too much exaggerated language to apply solely to the ancient high priest, but more appropriate for the "great high priest," the Son of God. The expressions "last end of the indignation" and "the end" (v. 19) as well "when the transgressors are come to the full" (v. 23) seem more appropriate when applied to the end of this age (see 1 Tim. 4:1 and following; 2 Tim. 3:1 and following). The same is true of "it shall be for many day" (v. 26).

IV. THE HISTORICAL CONCLUSION (Dan. 8:27)

Daniel was "done in," as a more literal translation would state in quite modern-sounding phraseology. After being laid aside for a while he went back to his work, evidently still pondering the meaning of what he wrote (cf. 1 Peter 1:10-12).

The events in Judah during the days of Antiochus have real applications to the church in the world today.

1. In the first place, it should be noted that Antiochus was only the instrument of affliction. The real source was in the apostasy from their faith and in the other sins of the Jewish people. They had become spiritually soft and interested mainly in ease and pleasure. His smooth speech and persuasive flatteries won them over too easily. Numerous elements among them were anxious to secure the popularity and honor he offered if they would conform to the pagan ways he was introducing. His was a time of conformity not unlike our own.

2. Observe further that one of the chief evils for which God allowed them this suffering was the secularization of their religion. A Greek-style gymnasium, with its offensive nakedness, was set up in Jerusalem so the youth could learn the pagan ways of Greece. They imitated Grecian styles and in every way tried to become less Jewish and more Greek. There was greater interest in Greek literature, foreign travel, and Greek philosophy than in study of the ancient Hebrew language and the Holy Scriptures. Some went so far as to deny their circumcision. Even high priests cast aside their Hebrew names for Greek names. These same religious leaders ostracized and opposed the loyal adherents to the old faith, castigating them as out of date and standing in the way of progress. Religion became only an instrument of state—its holy offices to be bought and sold for money.

3. The spirit that brought on the "indignation" was what today would have been called a "liberal" or "broad-minded" spirit. It is the spirit that stole from the churches of our land most of its Bible-focused centers of learning in the name of liberal arts several generations ago.

He would be foolish indeed who did not discern the parallels with our own days and feel something of a shiver of fright on account of it!

Take another look at the response of Daniel to his visions and the angelic interpretation. He was "done in"—greatly weakened in body by what he saw. He was full of grief that the lessons of their exile would not fully cure them of their spiritual adultery. He knew the grief of concern for the calamities of soul in other people.

4. Daniel's response shows that he really believed in his prophecies. And though he says "none understood it," we may be sure that he knew the general nature of the interpretation, for the angel made a great deal very plain. This should be somewhat of a guide to the proper attitude toward the study of prophecy today. We cannot understand all of it. We do not know "the day nor the hour" of our Lord's second advent, but we do know that He is coming!

9

Daniel 9:1-23

A Story of an Immediate Answer to Prayer

I. The Historical Setting of the Prophecy (Dan. 9:1-2)

II. The Exemplary Prayer of the Prophet (Dan. 9:3-19)

III. The Angelic Messenger Who Answered the Prayer (Dan. 9:20-23)

When a little knowledge of divine things brings confusion to the minds of some, they throw up their hands and resign from all effort at further understanding; leaving it for the "experts" to consider. This is especially true of the study of prophecy where a truly comprehensive knowledge of the Bible is necessary for full understanding. Paul's message to the Bereans was concerning Old Testament prophecies fulfilled in Jesus Christ (Acts 17:2-3). It was these Bereans who "were more noble . . . in that they received the word with all readiness of mind, and searched the scriptures daily, whether those things were so" (Acts 17:11). They were willing to pay the price in study effort. Precisely on that account "many of them believed."

In contrast to the Bereans there are others who make up their minds and set forth comprehensive pronouncements about the course of the future on the basis of very incomplete study. The best way is simply to continue studying, in prayer waiting for the leading of God. "The *Lord* giveth wisdom. . . . He layeth up sound wisdom for the *righteous*" (Prov. 2:6-7). His spirit must illuminate the understanding. A little more observation of human nature and of the ways of God helps much. When opinions are reached in this manner, there will be a humble spirit in the presentation of views that will stifle unnecessary controversy and promote Christian fellowship rather than hinder it.

Let Daniel's own example, then, be our guide as we further study the prophecies.

The chapter before us devotes 2 verses to the historical setting; 22 verses to a prayer of Daniel for himself, his people, and his country; and 4 verses to an answer to the prayer in the form of the most comprehensive chronological prophecy in the entire Bible. From the standpoint of doctrine, especially the unfolding in the New Testament of the four-verse prophecy with which the section closes, the prediction is most important. In the interest of placing emphasis where it belongs, a whole chapter of these expositions shall be devoted to the prayer and a whole chapter to its answer.

I. THE HISTORICAL SETTING OF THE PROPHECY
(Dan. 9:1-2)

In the first year of Darius the son of Ahasuerus, of the seed of the Medes, which was made king over the realm of the Chaldeans; in the first year of his reign I Daniel understood by books the number of the years, whereof the word of the Lord came to Jeremiah the prophet, that he would accomplish seventy years in the desolations of Jerusalem (Dan. 9:1-2).

The first year of Darius was the year 539-538 B.C. This puts the events of chapter 9 in the neighborhood of 67 years after Daniel was taken captive from Jerusalem at its first subjugation by Nebuchadnezzar in the summer of 605 B.C. It would have been about 60 years from the captivity of King Jehoiakim and his priestly subject, Ezekiel, who were taken to Babylon in the year 598 B.C. It was a bit less than 50 years after the complete destruction of the city in the summer of 586 B.C. This explains Daniel's interest in the prophecies of Jeremiah concerning 70 years of "desolations" for Jerusalem at this particular time and his interest in the "books" of prophetic Scripture in general.

The passage of greatest interest to Daniel was undoubtedly Jeremiah 25:11-12. After naming Nebuchadnezzar as the king who would come against the Jews, the passage reads, "And this whole land shall be a desolation, and an astonishment; and these nations shall serve the king of Babylon seventy years. And it shall come to pass, when seventy years are accomplished, that I will punish the king of Babylon, and that nation, saith the Lord, for their iniquity." Now Daniel must have been persuaded that the 70 years were now up—not almost over, but finished—for the king of Babylon had already been destroyed; and Cyrus, with Darius as his lieutenant, was reigning instead. On the basis of these calculations, Daniel would have concluded that Jeremiah's "seventy years" were to be taken as an approximate number, not an exact one, for actually a year or two less than 70 had passed by since the initial subjugation of Jerusalem by Nebuchadnezzar.

But there were other prophecies, especially one by Isaiah, made a century and a half before, concerning the restoration of the Jews from their captivity in Babylon to their homeland. Here are the famous words: Speaking of the Lord, Isaiah says: "that confirmeth the word of his servant, and performeth the counsel of his messengers; that saith to Jerusalem, Thou shalt be inhabited; and to the cities of Judah, Ye shall be built . . . that saith of Cyrus, He is my shepherd, and shall perform all my pleasure: even saying to Jerusalem: Thou shalt be built; and to the temple, Thy foundation shall be laid. Thus saith the Lord to his anointed, to Cyrus" (Isa. 44:26, 28; 45:1). Here the restoration of the Jews to their own country, the rebuilding of both their cities and their temples are predicted. Isaiah had even given the name of Cyrus, the very Persian king whose recent victories had brought about the fulfillment of Jeremiah's prophecy about Babylon. There were gaps in information in both Jeremiah's and Isaiah's predictions. Jeremiah, for example, had not said explicitly that Jerusalem should be rebuilt, nor that the Jews would be sent home *immediately* after the destruction of Babylon. Besides, Daniel might justifiably have wondered if the beginning of the prophetic 70 years might not be 586, when the temple and the city were burned. If so, there were in the neighborhood of at least 20 years before the restoration might occur. All this surely filled the prophet with a breathless expectancy.

When, in Jeremiah's time, the captivity was still only a prophecy, the prophet insisted that among the causes of the coming judgment was the fact that while people were placing great stock by their elaborate ritual and newly refurnished temple, they were not heeding their prophets. Not only did they fail to "speak the truth" (Jer. 9:5), but they were "not valiant for the truth" (Jer. 9:3). Worst of all, "the word of the Lord" was "unto them a reproach; they have no delight in it" (Jer. 6:10). Bible study was not a joy but a task; not a pleasure but a duty; not a delight but a burden! It took the wounds of the captivity to teach them some love for the truth and some interest in prayer. But not so Daniel; this man, perplexed by his vision, turned to the Word, "the books," and having "understood ... set my face unto the Lord God, to seek by prayer."

II. THE EXEMPLARY PRAYER OF THE PROPHET (Dan. 9:3-19)

Some portions of Scripture are creations of art. Like beautiful poems, paintings, gems, and statuary they must be seen whole to be appreciated. This portion of chapter 9, one of the lengthiest prayers reported in Scripture, is such a gem of literature. One really ought to read it several times to capture some of the beauty before attempting analysis of individual verses and words.

This particular prayer had an important place in the working out of the eternal plan of God. It is a principle that God not only ordains *ends* but *means* as well. God had foreseen and predestined the restoration (see especially Isa. 42:24-25; 43:14-15; 48:9-11; Jer. 49:17-20). But restoration was not without conditions. It was necessary that there be previous repentance and supplication (2 Chron. 6:36-39). In this respect the restoration of old was unlike the final restoration of the Jews which will apparently take place while they are yet in unbelief. Says God, "I will yet be inquired of by the house of Israel, to do it for them; I will increase them with men like a flock" (Ezek. 36:37). The restoration was not to come until there was "going and weeping" to "seek the Lord their God," and they should be prepared to say, "Come, let us join ourselves to the Lord" (Jer. 50:4-5, 20).

This prayer reveals the source of its strength; it shows on the part of its author his knowledge and appreciation of God. Daniel was bold to remind God that the city of Jerusalem, then lying in ruins, was "called by thy name," as likewise the Jewish people (vv. 18-19). This reminded God that His reputation was involved in the fortunes of the city and its people. The names of God, furthermore, are, as many names in Scripture, an indication of character. Daniel addressed his

Lord first as *Lord* God (v. 3, Heb. *Adonai Elohim*). *Adonai* means essentially master-lord in the old sense of the word—one's ruler. It emphasizes the sovereign rights of God; commonly God's name in relation to creations, preservation and providence. *Elohim* is the usual word for God. *Elohim* is a plural form, conveying the idea of His immensity. Daniel also called Him *the LORD my God* (v. 4, Heb. *Jehovah Elohim*). LORD, in the Authorized Version, all in capital letters, always translates Jehovah. Thus Daniel recognized God as the self-existent source of all being, the one who keeps promise with Abraham (see, Exod. 3:13-14; 6:1-8). Nine times the name Lord, *Adonai,* appears in the passage, showing that above everything else Daniel acknowledged God's sovereign rights, His power to do as He pleases. This is the primary confession of believers in all ages: "that Jesus Christ is Lord, to the glory of God the Father" (Phil. 2:11; Rom. 10:9-10).

Daniel's fervent reference to many of the attributes of his God shows even more in what knowledge and respect he held Him. He is "the great and dreadful God" (v. 4). His God, like Isaiah's, was "high and lifted up" before whose awful majesty the most exalted of God's whole creation can only cover their feet and faces while they cry "Holy, Holy, Holy" (Isa. 6:1 and following). Yet this dread majesty is matched by a compassion that keeps covenant "and mercy to them that love him, and to them that keep his commandments" (v. 4, cf. Exod. 20:5-6). These seeming opposites are really one, having their unity in God's holiness. That God is not only holy in character but righteous in His actions is admitted (vv. 7, 16). And Daniel in bold familiarity, born of long association, reminds his God of His reputation for "mercies and forgivenesses" (v. 9).

Without any particular effort to achieve logical arrangement of the various elements, let us view this prayer as a model prayer, and see where the path may lead. More than once the disciples asked our Lord to teach them to pray. In each case He gave examples and illustrations rather than instructions of a "theoretical" or "propositional sort" (Matt.

6:5-18; Luke 11:1-13).

A. In the first place, prayer is seen to be a wholesome lifelong spiritual exercise. In chapter 6 Daniel is seen to have risked his life to maintain his regular devotions. A comparison of Daniel 6:1-10 with 9:1-3 shows that his thrice daily prayer habit was tested at about the same time as this lengthy prayer. Daniel was now a very old man. For nearly 70 years he had maintained his watching and waiting vigils. During this time he had been subject to extreme temptation. The previous chapters are the story of those temptations. "Wealth, luxury, splendour, authority have not hurt his soul. How marvelous, how exceptional!" (Lang). The truth and the people of God are still uppermost in his thoughts. The holy city Jerusalem, although he had not seen it since childhood, the temple now in ruins, and the poor Jews of the dispersion are still his concern—precisely because they were God's. During these years Daniel had kept himself "unspotted from the world" and unspoiled by the subtle temptations of a luxurious court by this absorbtion in the things of God.

B. Daniel's prayer was marked with fierce determination. "I set my face unto the Lord God, to seek by prayer," he says (v. 3). It reminds us of the Lord, who when the time of His death came near "steadfastly set his face to go to Jerusalem" (Luke 9:51). Isaiah, prophetically describing that determination, places these words in the Lord's mouth: "For the Lord God will help me; therefore shall I not be confounded: therefore have I set my face like a flint, and I know that I shall not be ashamed" (Isa. 50:7).

Daniel's tenacity of purpose was the result of real appreciation of a desperate situation. Why should the new administration now replacing the Babylonians give the Jews any more kind attention than to a lost file-folder in the old Babylonian archives? Why should the insignificant descendants of captives from a small nation far away receive the attention of the mighty Persians? Furthermore, Daniel knew that his people had been but little improved by their sufferings. Perhaps the lonely years had only destroyed their hope and faith. And as he was to see (and probably already knew), the very hosts of wicked angels were arrayed against any restoration (Dan. 10:12-13, 20).

C. Related to his determination was <u>importunity</u>, or intensity of spirit. There is fervor breathed into the tenor of the whole passage. This aged prayer-warrior entered into his closet, and having shut the door, began "to seek" (v. 3). The very word implies intensity. W. C. Stevens has suggested that four degrees of progressive intensity are indicated. First there is "prayer" (v. 3), *general address.* This is surpassed by "supplications" or *pressing intreaties.* This is augmented in the third place "with fasting," temporary letting go of physical necessities. Perhaps the fervent old saint simply forgot to eat in his importunity. The fasting was overpassed, fourthly, when, laying aside his near-royal robes of high office, he made his prayer in "sackcloth, and ashes." These expressed *utter unworthiness and extreme need.* "He who *feels* that he has no personal claim (not merely admits it theoretically, as a matter of doctrine) will the more earnestly beg for help. One who believes he has a right, a claim, goes to his bank with quietness, with a sense of title. He takes for granted that he will receive without trouble what is his own. Not so the *suppliant*" (Lang). The suppliant comes with fervent supplication, crying both distinctly and often.

D. The importunity was in part a natural fruit of <u>humility</u>, or a sense of unworthiness, to which reference has just been made. Daniel had been honored by men as no Jew of his time; not even the captive kings and their sons had been so honored. God had exalted him greatly in making him the recipient of the great revelations and the seer of magnificant visions. With them had come no "thorn in the flesh" as with Paul, lest he be "exalted above measure" (2 Cor. 12:7). Yet there is not the slightest suggestion of pride. Not a hint of being puffed up. He still regards himself as a sinner, made of no different clay from that of other men, claiming that to him as to his brethren "belongeth confusion of face" (v. 8).

E. The most prominent feature of Daniel's prayer, preliminary to all supplication and intercession, was confession.

> And I prayed unto the Lord my God, and made my confession, and said, O Lord, the great and dreadful God, keeping the covenant and mercy to them that love him, and to that keep his commandments; we have sinned, and have committed iniquity, and have done wickedly, and have rebelled, even by departing from thy precepts and from thy judgments (Dan. 9:4-5).

Though the word for "confession" is rendered to "give thanks" and so forth, in many other passages, the peculiar Hebrew form used here is usually given the sense of confession as regards sin (for example, Lev. 5:5, "confess that he hath sinned").

Here as elsewhere confession is primarily toward God. Though we may harm others by our sins, and though we may greatly injure ourselves, sin is ultimately and mainly against the Creator who made us to bring Him glory. So Daniel addressed all his remarks about sin in such a way as to make it clear that it was "the great and dreadful God" whose honor was involved.

For good relations Christians are told to confess their *faults* one to another (James 5:16), their *sins* are against God and are to be confessed to Him alone. This they may do in complete confidence that they are forgiven (1 John 1:9—2:2).

The words for Daniel's own and the Jews' offenses against the Lord are in themselves an instructive study. They had "sinned" (v. 5). Translated also to err, neglect, fail, it emphasizes the falling short (Rom. 3:23) of God's high purposes. They had secondly, "committed iniquity" (v. 5), "done wrong" (RSV), "dealt perversely" (ASV), or they had "incurred guilt" in the sense of obligation to pay for what they had done. God is keeping books and bringing every deed into judgment. Thirdly, they had "done wickedly" or engaged in passionate rebellion against God.

Daniel adds a fourth, "and have rebelled," and a fifth, "by departing." These are some of the very strongest words of the

Hebrew language to express the idea of sin. Furthermore they cover the whole range of sin. Daniel was willing to call the thing by its right name.

Their sins consisted essentially in "departing" from God's "precepts and judgments." These are summarized in the Ten Commandments. Their sins were not complicated. In the years immediately before their captivity the prophet Jeremiah had laid them all bare. They were things like murder (Jer. 2:34), covetousness (Jer. 6:13), adultery and fornication (Jer. 5:7-8), lying (Jer. 5:30-31, 9:5), treachery (Jer. 9:8), Sabbath breaking (Jer. 17:21-22 and context), stealing (Jer. 7:9), and others. Every one of the Ten Commandments, especially that against idolatry, was being broken every day until, as the Scripture says, "there was no remedy" (2 Chron. 36:16).

> Neither have we hearkened unto thy servants the prophets, which spake in thy name to our kings, our princes, and our fathers, and to all the people of the land (Dan. 9:6).

The most adequate commentary on this verse is the rest of the Old Testament. The author of the books of Chronicles, written long afterward in the period of the Restoration gives a summary of it all at 2 Chronicles 36:14-20.

It should be noted that though the leaders—kings, princes, priests and others—are singled out for special mention here and in the prophets as being guilty of the sins which led to the destruction of the Jewish commonwealth, Daniel makes it very clear that all the people were guilty. Note Jeremiah's analysis: "A wonderful and horrible thing is committed in the land; the prophets prophesy falsely, and the priests bear rule by their means; and my people love to have it so" (Jer. 5:30-31). "My people love to have it so!" It is always like this. People usually find in their rulers what they demand in them.

Daniel continues his confession—having already mentioned the guilt of kings, princes, fathers, people (v. 6)—as follows:

> O Lord, righteousness belongeth unto thee, but unto us con-

fusion of faces, as at this day; to the men of Judah, and to the inhabitants of Jerusalem, and unto all Israel, that are near, and that are far off, through all the countries whither thou hast driven them, because of their trespass that they have trespassed against thee. O Lord, to us belongeth confusion of face, to our kings, to our princes, and to our fathers, because we have sinned against thee. Yea, all Israel have transgressed thy law, even by departing that they might not obey thy voice ... (Dan. 9:7-8, 11).

We have seen that Daniel's model prayer was exemplary of his daily practice; that it was with determination, importunity, humility; and that a major subject was confession of sins. Now the impression is laid heavily upon us that—

F. The model "pray-er" associated himself completely with his people. How easy it might have been for Daniel to disassociate himself in thought, sympathy, affection, and confession from his people. But this is not the force of his words: *"we* have sinned" (v. 5), "neither have *we* hearkened" (v. 6), "unto *us* confusion of faces" (v. 7), "neither have *we* obeyed" (v. 10), "therefore the curse is poured upon *us* (v. 11), "he spake against *us*" (v. 12), and so forth. Most striking in view of his prayer life and study of the Word is the admission, "yet made we not our prayer before the Lord our God, that we might turn from our iniquities, and understand thy truth" (v. 13). This feature of Daniel's prayer points to a fact of life which we are inclined to ignore or reject. This fact is that we are joined with our neighbors, family and others. What happens in a remote corner affects every one of us. Adam's sin brought a whole race to ruin; the single assassination on a obscure archduke in remote Sarajevo of a small country (Serbia) June 28, 1914, set off a great war that embroiled the whole world. The pastor or missionary who would help his people must truly associate himself with them. He must be one of them in life, thought, affection, and interest. Daniel makes us think of Him "who, although He existed in the form of God, did not regard equality with God a thing to be grasped, but emptied Himself taking the form of a bond-servant, and being made in the likeness of men" (Phil.

2:6-7 NASB).

G. Daniel's prayer was made in submission to the will and wisdom of God.

> Therefore hath the Lord watched upon the evil, and brought it upon us: for the Lord our God is righteous in all his works which he doeth: for we obeyed not his voice (Dan. 9:14).

Sometimes when we pray it is out of desperation—a desperation due to dissatisfaction with what life has given us. We complain that our rights have been overrun or we have received less than we have deserved. Full of self-pity and self-interest we run to God and complain against Him. Let us always remember that "the Lord our God is righteous in all his works which he doeth."

H. While confession is the major burden of the prayer, **the purpose of it was to make petition and intercession.** Petition (prayer for one's self) and intercession (prayer for others) are really joined in this prayer, for Daniel's interests and those of his people are the same.

The burden of Daniel's prayer was request for the restoration of his country, its people, its land, its worship at the temple (see vv. 16-21). There are those who wish to interpret the answer of the prayer (I refer to the angelic oracle of vv. 24-27 with which the chap. ends) as having really small reference to the Jewish people, their land and temple, supposing it to refer to the New Testament church. Contrariwise the prayer is especially clear. Every word of it relates to "thy city Jerusalem, thy holy mountain [Zion] . . . Jerusalem and thy people" (v. 16).

The reasons supplied by Daniel, for he does carry on a kind of argument, are: 1) that God's own people are a reproach (v. 16); 2) God is a merciful God (v. 18); and 3) God's own reputation is at stake, for everyone knows that both the people and the city are called by the Lord's name (v. 19); and hence the request is made for God's own sake (v. 19). It is not far different from Moses' prayer-argument in a similar situation (Exod. 32:10-14).

A final point about the prayer must be made: The people and city which Daniel associates with the LORD as "*thy* city and *thy* people ... called by *thy name*" appear to have been disowned by God at the time Daniel prayed. The people were still in disobedience. God referred to them not as His own but Daniel's (v. 24).

III. THE ANGELIC MESSENGER WHO ANSWERED THE PRAYER (Dan. 9:20-23)

And while I was speaking, and praying, and confessing my sin and the sin of my people Israel, and presenting my supplication before the Lord my God for the holy mountain of my God; yea, while I was speaking in prayer, the man Gabriel, whom I had seen in the vision at the beginning, being caused to fly swiftly, touched me about the time of the evening oblation. And he informed me, and talked with me, and said, O Daniel, I am now come forth to give thee skill and understanding. At the beginning of thy supplications the commandment came forth, and I am come to shew thee; for thou art greatly beloved: therefore consider the matter, and consider the vision.

This section focuses on Gabriel the messenger (or angel) of God. There is only a little information about Gabriel in the Bible. He appeared in human form, as apparently angels always do, for he is said to have the "appearance of a man" (8:15). The word for man here is *gaber* (sometimes *geber*). Related to the word "to be strong," it means valiant male, one of heroic proportions, or a noble person. Though sent to comfort and inform Daniel and speaking with simplicity and great kindness, on each occasion of his appearance the prophet was left troubled and greatly fearful. This suggests there was something about Gabriel which inspired awe.

What may be of greater importance is that God sent off His messenger at the beginning of Daniel's prayers, presumably at the beginning of the day: "At the beginning of thy supplications the commandment came [went] forth" (v. 23). This was before the prophet even expressed his prayer in words.

A careful look at Daniel's report of Gabriel's interruption of the prayer will supply a kind of final summary of this exemplary prayer. It is also a fine guide for private prayers today. Twice Daniel says Gabriel came "while I was speaking" (vv. 20-21). God knows men's thoughts, even when they are "afar off" (Ps. 139:2). Yet there is value in expressing prayer "out loud" when we are able to do so. Prayers may even be written. Silent prayer tends to be wandering. Rational beings should put their thoughts in order, especially when petitioning the Lord of all.

Daniel says he was "speaking, and *praying*" (v. 20), "speaking in *prayer*" (v. 21). Most of the time no word for pray or prayer is used in the Old Testament when men are said to talk to God. The essential idea is to intercede, either for one's self or for someone or something else. The idea of laying a person or matter before God is central. Many prayers should be simply that, saying, as it were, "Lord, please look at this situation and act as You know best." A clear example is the prayer of Acts 4:24-30.

What is to be understood and what is to be gained from the fact that Daniel was "greatly beloved" of God (v. 23)? The word beloved means lovely, object of desire, delightful (food), costly (raiment), precious (stones or metals), and it is a passive participle. So Daniel is not designated as loving but loved, not desiring but desirable. The word "greatly" simply conveys the plural of greatness which the Hebrew word requires. Three times Gabriel so describes Daniel (cf. 10:11, 19). The moral qualities of Daniel on display throughout this book made him lovely to God, and the Bible associates him with Noah and Job (Ezek. 14:14, 20). These qualities were carried with him into his prayers. Surely there are such saintly aged persons among us today.

10

Daniel 9:24-27

The Prophecy of the Seventy Weeks

I. The Special Character of the Seventy Weeks (Dan. 9:24)

II. The First Sixty-Nine of the Weeks (Dan. 9:25)

III. The Lapse of Time "After" Sixty-Nine Weeks but Before the Seventieth (Dan. 9:26)

IV. The Seventieth Week (Dan. 9:27)

These four verses are a unique paragraph in biblical prophecy. All of the Book of Daniel is rather special in the intimacy of its young, then aged, author—a "man greatly beloved" of God. But these four verses are unique even in this unusual biblical book. This has long been recognized. The famous Jewish historian, Flavius Josephus of Jerusalem, whose long life began during the time of Jesus' ministry, wrote this about Daniel 9:24-27:

> It is fit to give an account of what this man did, which it is most admirable to hear; for he was so happy as to have strange revelations made to him, and those as to one of the greatest of the prophets, insomuch that while he was alive he had the esteem and applause both of the kings and of the multitude: and now he is dead, he retains a remembrance that will never fail, for the several books that he wrote and left behind him are still read by us till this time; and from them we believe that Daniel conversed with God; for he *did not only prophesy of future events, as did the other prophets, but he also determined the time of their accomplishment* (italics added).

We know that at about the time of the birth of Jesus there were people all over the world looking for the coming of some sort of cosmic change. In Israel there was a crescendo of "apocalypic" excitement among common people outside of the parties of national leadership—that is, outside of the Pharisee and Sadducee parties. There were those then who were allowing God only a generation in which to send the Messiah. To borrow a term from today—there were those who were furnishing "a count down" for Armageddon.

But there was a wiser, smaller group, who had essentially the same theology as they looked for the Messiah of David or of Israel. They were not a party, just sane, informed, faithful, believing Bible students and worshipers. Of these Joseph and Mary (Matt. 1:18-25; Luke 1:26-56; 2:19-24), the parents of John the Baptist (Luke 1:5-80), and the aged Simeon and Anna (Luke 2:25-38) are examples. A bit later are Joseph of Arimathea (Luke 23:50-52) and perhaps Nicodemus. Simeon was "looking for the consolation of Israel." Anna was one of a larger group of "all them that looked for redemption in Jerusalem" (Luke 2:38). John's parents, Zacharias and Elizabeth, were "walking in all the commandments and ordinances of the Lord blameless" (Luke 1:6). Joseph of Arimathea was "a good and righteous man ... who was looking for the kingdom of God" (Luke 23:50-51).

David L. Cooper (though he wrote 30 years ago) speaks to our present situation:

> The first century situation should teach us a serious lesson. The group which clustered around such people as Symeon and the prophetess Anna seem to have been very cautious, taking only what the Word said and refusing to indulge in extravagant, sensational, fantastic interpretations of the Scriptures. On the other hand, there was another group of prophetic students, who produced the apocalyptic of the first century and who indulged in many wild and sensational theories. Of course, there were many people then, like the masses today, who simply lived upon the fantastic and extravagant theories of sensational teachers. This group doubtless brought the study of prophecy into disrepute. It takes no wide stretch of the imagination to believe that the Sadducean, materialistic [and rationalistic] party was driven into their cold, philosophical isolation by the effervescent, sensational, prophetic teaching of those indulging in this extreme, fantastic interpretation of prophecy.

Cooper goes on to remind us that God fulfills prophecy as written not as speculated upon.

Of great practical blessing for Daniel, and by way of an encouraging precedent to us, is the fact that the answer was immediate—while he was still on his knees in prayer. In verse 23 Gabriel reports that he was commanded to come as soon as the prayer began, evidently consuming some time in coming to speak to Daniel. God has said there would be days like that, "And it shall come to pass, that before they call, I will answer; and while they are yet speaking, I will hear" (Isa. 65:24). As we shall see in the next chapter, God sometimes responds differently, for sometimes He delays His answers, for our good. But He may, as an encouragement to faith, and as a necessary part of answer, give His response immediately.

Since God is sovereign in such matters, men must be submissive.

Gabriel told the prophet that whereas Jeremiah had predicted 70 years of desolations for Jerusalem, God had still another prophetic period in mind for Israel. This period would be one of 70 *sevens* of years (the Hebrew word for week is really a word meaning "a seven"). The force of comparison of "seventy years" (v. 2) with "seventy weeks [sevens]" (v. 24) is in effect that God is revealing a new period of God's dealing with the Holy People exactly seven times as long as the predicted, and now fulfilled, prophecy by Jeremiah of 70 years of desolation of Jerusalem.

Though there are some who demur, the preponderance of opinion among scholars is that these weeks are weeks of years. What are the reasons for this? The word "week" automatically brings a period of seven days before the mind of English-speaking people. The reasons are as follows. 1) The Hebrew word for "week" is literally "a seven." It could be a seven of hours, days, years, or of marbles. Context has to determine. 2) As comparison of Daniel 9:2 with 2 Chronicles 36:21 shows (cf. Jer. 25:11), a week of years was already on the prophet's mind. 3) There was a well-known "seven" or week of years familiar to all Hebrews for it was in their law (Exod. 23:10-11; Lev. 25:3-9; see also Gen. 29:27-28). 4) In the very next chapter, Daniel, when he wished to make it clear that he was referring to a week of days, specified it. In Daniel 10:2-3, where the word "seven" appears, the Hebrew word for days follows, a seven *of days*. Evidently it was Daniel's custom to speak thus, for obviously he did not fast for 21 years! 5) Likewise the facility this gives to interpretation of the many references elsewhere in the Bible to half of this week as three and one-half years is an argument for it.

All interpreters must resolutely hold to the fact that the 70 "sevens" of years were determined upon Daniel's "people" and "holy city" (v. 24). To apply the prophecy to something else is surely an error. Furthermore, it seems likely that the 70 "sevens" of years apply only to periods when "the people" are dwelling in the "holy city."

Once it is agreed that the prophecy relates to Jerusalem and to Jews; the field of investigation is narrowed immensely and possibilities of understanding are enlarged.

Perhaps the best way for anyone to begin his studies of a difficult passage like this one is to read it slowly, think of the context as he reads, and see what the obvious meaning seems to be. Insofar as the circumstances of treatment in a book of this type allows, we shall do just that, verse by verse, following the American Standard Version (1901).

I. The Special Character of the Seventy Weeks (Dan. 9:24)

> Seventy weeks are decreed upon thy people and upon thy holy city, to finish transgression, and to make an end of sins, and to make reconciliation for iniquity, and to bring in everlasting righteousness, and to seal up vision and prophecy, and to anoint the most holy [marg. a most holy place] (Dan. 9:24).

Besides announcing the coming period of 490 years on the Jews and Jerusalem, the angel states *what* God is going to do in the period (not *after* it, but *in* it). It is in the next three verses that we are told *how* these things shall come to pass. Six things are to take place concerning Daniel's "people," Israel, and their "city," Jerusalem:

A. "To finish transgression." Daniel had been confessing the rebellious breaches of the divine law. Within this period these transgressions are to come to an end. The Hebrew word has no connection with atonement, as advocates of a "church" interpretation suppose, but rather to restrain, cause to cease (as the rain, Gen. 8:2). The disobedience of these people is to cease; an age of obedience is to be ushered in.

B. "To make an end of sins." A literal translation is "to seal up sins." As in the Book of Job where it is said of God, He "sealeth up the stars" so that they do not shine (Job 9:7), and as cold weather "sealeth up the hand of every man" so that he cannot continue his accustomed daily labor (Job 37:7), so in this period of 70 weeks of years, the sins of

Daniel's people are to be brought under full restraint. The same seems to be the idea of sealing Satan in the pit—to bring his activities to an end (Rev. 20:1 and following). Sins are related to transgressions as failures are consequent upon a rebellious attitude.

C. "To make reconciliation for iniquity." Israel will make things right with God again when they are again in their land, "in that day" of His second appearing, "they shall look unto me whom they have pierced" (see Zech. 12:10; cf. Rev. 1:7), and shall repent (Jer. 50:4-5 and 17-20 should be read at this point). "In those days, and in that time, saith Jehovah, the iniquity of Israel shall be sought for, and there shall be none; and the sins of Judah, and they shall not be found: for I will pardon them whom I reserve" (Jer. 50:20).

The previous three matters to be effected during the 490 years are negative: the settlement of their sin problem; the second group of three have to do with the establishment of positive righteousness among them, not imputed righteousness but personal righteousness and national moral integrity.

D. "To bring in everlasting righteousness." This will be effected by an inward moral transformation within the people, writing the law of God in their hearts (Jer. 31:33-40).

E. "To seal up vision and prophecy [margin and Heb., **prophet**]." When there is no more sin to correct, the disciplinary words of the prophets will cease to be needed. This is specifically declared at Jeremiah 31:34.

F. "To anoint the most holy [margin, **a most holy place**]." There is more agreement among commentators with regard to the interpretation of this phrase than might be expected. Most of them agree that the language specifies that with the ending of sinning among Daniel's people and the bringing in of righteousness, a new Jewish temple shall be anointed, that is, set aside for divine worship. Mount Zion will be crowned with a new temple, of which the tabernacle and the succession of temples of old were but shadows. The glory-presence of the Lord will return (Ezek. 43:1-7). One passage even seems to hint that God will create anew the pillar of cloud by day and the pillar of fire by night (Isa. 4:5). The ritual, since the death of our Lord put an end to sacrifices forever, will presumably be different. However, "The latter glory of this house will be greater than the former, says the Lord of hosts, and in this place I shall give peace" (Hag. 2:9 NASB).

II. The First Sixty-Nine of the Weeks (Dan. 9:25)

> Know therefore and discern, that from the going forth of the commandment to restore and to build Jerusalem unto the anointed one, the prince, shall be seven weeks, and threescore and two weeks: it shall be built again, with street and moat, even in troublous times (Dan. 9:25).

There never has been but one common Christian interpretation of "the anointed one, the prince": that he is the Lord Jesus Christ. "Anointed" is the Hebrew word "Messiah," in Greek translation, *Christos;* Latin, *Christus;* hence, English, Christ. The word "prince" is a designation entirely proper to the Saviour (see the familiar words of Isa. 9:6-7; cf. Luke 1:32-33).

Now, therefore, we see two periods, one of seven sevens (49 years) to be followed by another of 62 sevens (434 years), 483 years in all, were to expire between the giving of a decree to restore the Jewish city of Jerusalem and the appearance of Christ. The decree is one made in heaven, of course, but manifest on earth by some king's announcement. An examination of the evidence leads to the conclusion that only one decree reported in the Old Testament fits the specifications as a "commandment to restore and to build Jerusalem." This was the one made by the Persian king Artaxerxes Longimanus (465-423 B.C.) in the year 445 (perhaps 444) B.C. and executed by Nehemiah. The story is told in the first two chapters of Nehemiah. Alva J. McClain has put the matter well:

> This "commandment" by a large number of interpreters, has been identified with the decrees issued by Cyrus, Darius, and

Artaxerxes, recorded in the Book of Ezra. But these decrees without any exception have to do with the building of the *Temple,* not the city. Let the student read carefully Ezra 1:1-2; 4:1-5, 11-24; 6:1-5, 14-15; 7:11, 20, 27, and notice that in every case the decree concerns the "house of the Lord." But there is no authorization for the rebuilding of the city. And it is an interesting fact that the rebuilding of the Temple was stopped for a time because of accusations from Jewish enemies that the Jews were attempting without authority also to rebuild the *city* (Ezra 4:1-24).

True, the prophecy of Isaiah 44:28 seems at first glance to contradict McClain (who is citing the investigations of Sir Robert Anderson). The syntax of the obscure sentence is, however, best understood as meaning that God "that saith of Cyrus, He is my shepherd" is likewise the subject who says "of Jerusalem, She shall be built."

What events were to transpire during the first period of seven weeks (49 years) is not stated, but likely it was the completion of the Restoration city or city wall. Why it took so long is explained by several facts. The massive walls erected over the centuries on old Jebusite foundations by a succession of kings, David to Zedekiah, and many times enlarged and repaired, really had been broken down by Nebuchadnezzar's men. They were in wholly wrecked condition when Nehemiah and his men set out to rebuild them (Neh. 1:3; 2:3, 13, 17). The people were neither numerous nor especially ambitious, as the books of Ezra, Nehemiah and Malachi show. Furthermore, there were many opponents and several interruptions (Nehemiah).

There is no suggestion of any interval or gap between the 7- and the 62-week periods. I am acquainted with no convincing arguments for any break in the consecutive continuity of the prophecy before the end of the sixty-ninth week.

A bit of simple arithmetic shows how the prophecy was fulfilled. Seven times 69 is 483 years, the period from the decree of the Persian king to Messiah's presentation. The time from 445 to about 30 A.D., the end of Christ's career, is about 474 years (1 B.C. to A.D. 1 is one year). Knowing, as we do, that our knowledge of dates in those ages is only approximately certain, and that prophecies of time were not always exactly intended, the correspondence is close enough to demonstrate that Daniel really did predict the actual time of Messiah's appearance.

It is possible, however, that we may be able to refine the matter further. The New Testament seems to indicate that Christ only once officially presented himself to the Jews as their "Messiah-Prince," and that was at the beginning of the last week of His life in what is known as the "Triumphal Entry." Fulfilling the prediction that their "king" would come to them "just, and having salvation; lowly, and riding upon an ass" (Zech. 9:9, cf. Matt. 21:5-6), Jesus on that one occasion presented Himself to the nation as their promised king. Previously He had commanded His disciples not to proclaim Him as the Messiah (Matt. 16:20). He had previously steadfastly refused either to be made king or to act as their judge (John 6:15, Luke 12:13-14). But on this day He gave the instructions for his entrance to Jerusalem that led to His being proclaimed by the crowds as Son of David, the promised king who would come in Jehovah's name (Luke 19:28-38). As Jesus moved into sight of the city, some of the Pharisees complained and asked Him to rebuke His followers. Jesus answered them: "if these should hold their peace, the stones would immediately cry out" (Luke 19:40). This was clearly His presentation day. He apparently knew He was acting in God's will and thereby fulfilling Old Testament prophecy. No other understanding of these words seems adequate to explain the solemn intent.

Certain scholars have interpreted the 70 weeks of prophetic years on the basis of a 360-day year. Making full account of astronomical and chronological data, they have calculated that Daniel's prediction was carried out to the very day (Anderson, *The Coming Prince,* ably summarized for the lay reader by McClain, *Daniel's Prophecy of the Seventy Weeks*). The case is a strong one and is well presented.

III. The Lapse of Time "After" Seventy-Nine Weeks but Before the Seventieth (Dan. 9:26)

And after the threescore and two weeks shall the anointed one be cut off, and shall have nothing: and the people of the prince that shall come shall destroy the city and the sanctuary; and the end thereof shall be with a flood, and even unto the end shall be war; desolations are determined (Dan. 9:26).

It is crucial to understanding this portion of prophecy to note carefully that two events clearly indicated and separated by thirty-eight years of time, are introduced *after* the sixty-ninth week but *before* the seventieth. The text says "after" and the order of happenings requires "before." These two events are the cutting off of Messiah by death (about 30 A.D.) and the destruction of Jerusalem and its temple about 40 years later (70 A.D.) by the people (Roman) of the "coming" wicked prince Antichrist. There are competent interpreters of nearly every school of believing interpretation who insist that this coming prince is Antichrist, said to be "coming" because his coming has previously been clearly predicted in Daniel (chap. 7).

Some interpreters have been pressed by the language of the next verse, especially as interpreted by Paul, to look for fulfillment of the prophecy in the times of final Antichrist. If we then find *definite* periods of time indicated by the weeks then some period of time is passed over between the first week and the seventieth. Already in Christian antiquity the "eschatological" bearing of verse 27 was widely recognized. Thus, a lapse of time is introduced between the sixty-ninth and seventieth weeks—not arbitrarily by theologians, as is sometimes claimed, but exegetically by the very language of the text itself. This verse suggests, however, that continuing wars, invasions (flood) and desolations shall plague the city of Jerusalem until "the end." (Overwhelming catastrophe or distress of any kind is frequently designated as a "flood" in Scripture. See for example Ps. 32:6.)

IV. The Seventieth Week (Dan. 27)

And he shall make a firm covenant with many for one week: and in the midst of the week he shall cause the sacrifice and the oblation to cease; and upon the wing of abominations shall come one that maketh desolate; and even unto the full end, and that determined, shall wrath be poured out upon the desolate (Dan. 9:27).

This coming prince, the anti-Messiah, shall effect a seven-year league covenant with Daniel's people in their city (v. 24), people known in chapter 7 and chapter 8 as "the holy people." In the middle of it Antichrist shall break the league, and begin to persecute them, as his ancient prototype, Antiochus, did in the second century B.C.

It is beyond the scope of this study to treat fully the later biblical references to the two halves of this seventieth week. In His last great address, Jesus made reference to the "abomination" that marks its midpoint (see Matt. 24:15 and following). Paul's discussion of the "son of perdition" or "man of sin" (2 Thess., chap. 2) relates in part to the same event. The second half of this week is referred to in some of the other oracles of Daniel—the three and one-half times wherein the little horn persecutes the holy people (Dan. 7:25) and at least three times in the twelfth chapter (vv. 7, 11-12). Most importantly the seven years, halved into two periods and indicated in Revelation by such literary devices as three and one-half times, 1,260 days, 42 months, becomes important to the interpretation of that book, supplying the indispensible key to the futurist interpretation. This halved period is referred to no less than five times therein (see Rev. 11:2-3; 12:6, 14; 13:5).

These chronological data are bewildering to the beginning student of prophetic matters. One should beware of accepting uncritically everything that is said about them, but contrariwise, one should certainly approach their study with a hopeful, sanctified curiosity to understand the oracles of God.

The answer to his prayer was not what the prophet expected. How could he have expected it? He no doubt hoped that God would tell him that the exile would end and here restoration, complete, final, and forever would come at the end of the 70 years of Jeremiah's prediction. God answered with more light. With the light came not an end to effort and study; rather with new tasks, new problems, new duties, and above all with new strength.

A Survey of Interpretation of the Seventy Weeks

It should be clear that convinced as we may be of the general correctness of our views of this passage, there must be humility in the presence of others who with equal or greater piety and learning come to somewhat variant views. Some of these interpreters derive the very most Christ-honoring doctrine from these four verses—correct except that it does not seem to be supported by the passage.

Presuppositions brought to the passage count for much in interpreting it, but not quite everything, for though those who will not accept predictive prophecy see nothing of our Lord Jesus Christ's advent or advents in it, they are not the only ones who think it was all fulfilled long before His birth. Further, though many Christian interpreters have thought the prophecy relates to His first advent and was completely fulfilled at about that time, other believing interpreters have insisted that prophecy relates to both first and second advents. Nor do the interpreters simply line up along the lines of doctrines of the millennium or of dispensations or of covenants.

Let us examine some of these views and the bases of them.

(1) We will start with those who will not allow in their thinking the possibility that God could and did unveil some events of the future that human calculations could not foresee or guess. Most of these interpreters are at one—enough so that it is quite correct to refer to "the" critical-liberal view. The going forth of the command to restore and build Jerusalem with which the series of 490 years begins is the coming of the prophecy from God to Jeremiah—about 70 years of desolation of Jerusalem. Never mind that Jeremiah spoke

that word (see Jer. 25:1, 11-12; cf. Dan. 9:2) in about 606/5 B.C., the seven weeks (=49 years) must be counted from the ending of temple rites in 586 B.C. when Nebuchadnezzar destroyed Jerusalem. They must terminate at 539/8 B.C. when Cyrus of Persia allowed the rites to resume, as reported in the Book of Ezra. So from the command to an "anointed" one (Cyrus? or Joshua? or Zerubbabel?) is really 49 years, *period.* Then the second space, of 62 weeks or 434 years, starts. The 62 weeks end with the cutting off (execution) of a second anointed person (vv. 25 and 26). The RSV translation, especially the punctuation of verse 25, practically demands two anointed persons in the prophecy. This second anointed is the martyr high priest Onias III who was murdered at Antioch by a Jewish rival priest (2 Maccabees 4:23-28) about 170 B.C. The period was really only 369 years (65 years short), but the author of Daniel had only a vague idea of how long it was, actually writing the prophecy in about 165 B.C. The seventieth week all belongs to the period of seven or eight years after 170 B.C. when Antiochus Epiphanes, king of Syria, sought to suppress Judaism in Judea. There actually is considerable correspondence between Daniel 9:26-27 and the seven years of Antiochus' dealings with the Jews after about 170 B.C. For those futurist interpreters who are convinced that critical events of biblical history can be predictive, in a partial or vague way, of critical events of the future as ordered by God, this similarity poses no problem.

(2) A common believing Christian view holds that all six items to be accomplished (Dan. 9:24) were completed at our Lord's first advent. Some advocate that the weeks begin with the decree of Artaxerxes Longimanus in the twentieth year of his reign, April/May 445 B.C. (Neh. 1). A few work from the decree of Artaxerxes Longimanus (reigned 464-424 B.C.) in the seventh year of his reign, 458 B.C. (Ezra 7:1-28). A majority of all Christian writers except in recent past, count the end of the seven plus sixty-two weeks, that is, the sixty-ninth at the baptism of Jesus, the beginning of His messianic

work, in A.D. 26. This, by the commonly accepted chronology of this part of ancient history is exactly 483 years (69x7=483) if the start of the 70 weeks is 458 B.C. (Ezra 7:1-28). It is computed in the following manner: 458x26-1 (1 B.C. to A.D. 1 is only one year. There is no year, zero.) equals 483. After the three and one-half years of Jesus' ministry He is "cut off," that is, crucified, thereby "confirming" or effecting the covenant of redemption (Gen. 3:16) with "the many" and accomplishing the six items of Daniel 9:24. The three and one-half years of ministry and three and one-half years following, some say terminated by the martyrdom of Stephen bring the seventieth week and thereby the entire 490 years to a close. At this point God ends forever any special dealing with Daniel's people (Jews) and city (Jerusalem). The destruction of Jerusalem is a painful item for these interpreters since it came over 35 years after the close of the seventieth week in their counting. This has led some of this persuasion to assert that there is no definite termination date.

(3) Another group of interpreters agree theologically in main with the second view except for two details: a) the sevens symbolize indefinite periods of time. They are not even necessarily years. b) the periods of time indicated by 70, 7, 63 and 1 are neither definite nor proportional. The 7 weeks run from Cyrus' permission for Zerubbabel and Joshua to return (538 B.C., Ezra 1:1–2:2) to about 440 B.C., the 62 weeks run thence to Christ—no specific point in His life. The seventieth week includes the ministry of Christ and ends with the destruction of Jerusalem 40 years later.

(4) Because of reasons given earlier in this chapter, many interpreters of all schools (postmillennial, amillennial, premillennial and others, who have no interest in the millennium) have seen clearly that the events predicted in verse 27 belong to the end-times, when the course of the present age is coming to an end. How can Paul's words in 2 Thessalonians 2:3-12 and those of Jesus in all three versions of the Olivet Discourse (Matt. 24:15-31; Mark 13:14-27; Luke 21:20-28) fail to make this point? Even the liberal critical writers insist

on this, though they insist that the time for the consummation was supposed to be in Antiochus' time (170-164 B.C.) and that the author of Daniel (of 165 B.C.) was in error! So there are several views which terminate the weeks with the Antichrist and the Second Advent.

(5) C. F. Keil (of Keil and Delitzsch fame), though a warm-hearted evangelical, adopted the reading (that is, punctuation) basic to the liberal-critical view—a period mark after "seven weeks" (Dan. 9:25). The result for him was not, however, antisupernaturalist, for he was convinced regarding the six statements of verse 24 that "it thus appears that the termination of the 70 weeks coincides with the present course of the world." I think Keil's arguments on verse 24 are unbreakable and that the efforts to find their complete fulfillment at the time of our Lord's first advent are quite futile, both in detail and in aggregate. The fact that both Paul (2 Thess. 2) and Jesus (Olivet Discourse) give an eschatological interpretation of verse 26 is thus no problem to Keil. He boldly puts the fulfillment in the times of Antichrist. This is especially meaningful, for as one who believed in the replacement of Israel by the church, and an amillennialist, his faithful adherence to what seemed to him (and seems likewise to me) the final future reference of verses 24, 26 and 27, it would have been easier to take the ways out suggested by alternate but less supportable interpretations.

Dr. Keil is, I think, very much mistaken in tracing the 62 weeks through the course of the present age. That the seventieth is to be fulfilled in the last times, I agree. The weeks, then, do not designate precise numbers of years but only indefinite periods of time. Keil was too acute a thinker to commit Apollinarius' (and a host of others since—Irvingites, Seventh-Day Adventists, Russellites, overenthusiastic popular prophecy *experts*) error of date-setting.

Many of the views just described arose in Christian antiquity and are known today chiefly through the commentary on Daniel by Jerome (died A.D. 420). It is from this little-read source that the present writer learned of them.

Daniel 10:1–11:35

A Vision of God:

A Story of Delayed Answer to Prayer

I. The Circumstances of the Revelation (Dan. 10:1-4)

II. The Description of the Revelation and of its Effect (Dan. 10:5-9)

III. The Strengthening of the Prophet to Receive a Message (Dan. 10:10-12, 15-19)

IV. The Scope of the Prophecy (Dan. 10:14)

V. The Conflicts of the Angelic Messenger (Dan. 10:13, 20-21)

VI. Prophecy of the Immediate Future of Israel in Relation to the Nations (Dan. 11:1-35)

The careful student should read the last three chapters of the book as one before attempting to study the portion before us. These three chapters are really one section, comparable to one of the previous chapters, each of which is truly a unit. The previous chapters reporting Daniel's visions (7, 8, 9) each first relates an introductory vision of God, then describes its effects on the prophet. Next appear additional revelations and, finally, an interpretation of their meaning. Approximately the same takes place in this final section of three chapters. Chapter 10 records the initial vision; chapters 11 and 12 contain the main revelations and interpretations. Several distinct prophecies, or oracles, of Daniel begin with the date when the author received them (2:1; 7:1; 8:1; 9:1). The appearance of a date in the first verse of chapter 11 gives the impression that here also is the beginning of a new oracle. This, however, is a false impression, for it falls in the midst of a speech by the revealing angel begun in the preceding chapter.

The section for this present study includes the (1) initial vision, then (2) further revelations imparted by the angel concerning the future of Israel in intercourse with certain nations of antiquity. These matters culminate in the oppressions of Antiochus Epiphanes in the last half of the second century B.C. These events are now all a part of ancient history. Throughout these last three chapters of the book, God is, so to speak, "filling in the picture" sketched out in the prophecies of the earlier parts of the book.

There is nothing more natural than for men to desire to literally see God. Every occurrence of idolatry is an example of the possible misdirection of this desire, with consequent corruption of all that might be good in mankind.

I. THE CIRCUMSTANCES OF THE REVELATION
(Dan. 10:1-4)

In the third year of Cyrus king of Persia a thing was revealed unto Daniel, whose name was called Belteshazzar; and the thing was true, but the time appointed was long: and he understood the thing, and had understanding of the vision (Dan. 10:1).

The date, the third year of Cyrus, is very important. It explains why Daniel was in mourning. The rebuilding of the Jerusalem temple of the Lord had been interrupted. According to Ezra 1:1, and following, King Cyrus decreed that the Jews might return to their homeland in the first year of his reign. Less than two years later the foundation of the restoration temple was laid (Ezra, chap. 3). But immediately oppositions from renegade Jews in the vicinity stopped the work and discouraged the workmen (Ezra 4:4-5). Finally, the cessation of the building activity was decreed by Cambyses. And besides this, not many Jews had responded to the invitation to go home to Palestine.

There is probably no place in the entire Bible where there is more emphasis placed upon the absolute reliability of the reports and upon the absolute truth of the matters reported. "A thing was revealed," says the prophet. This means that the "word" or "message" (both more appropriate than "thing," as translation) was revealed from heaven. Not only so, the "thing [Heb., *matter*] was true." The accompanying miraculous signs were such as to render disbelief in the divine origin of the experiences and messages impossible. "The time appointed was long" is an obvious error of translation, for it should be that "the warfare was great" or even "the suffering was great." This means that these things came to Daniel in the midst of extreme physical and mental suffering. So, far from looking back upon his vision of the Godhead as a pleasant experience, he honestly could say that it almost killed him, and except for special strengthening, the experience would have killed him. But these very sufferings were part of the experience of divine presence which rendered the "matter" so unquestionably true. Daniel's words about understanding the "matter" or "vision" showed that Daniel had no great problem in understanding most of what he was told by the angel. Daniel 12:8, which says he "understood not," seems to relate only to the cryptic words immediately preceding.

In those days I Daniel was mourning three full weeks. I ate no pleasant bread, neither came flesh nor wine in my mouth, neither did I anoint myself at all, till three whole weeks were fulfilled. (Dan. 10:2-3).

There is not a hint that Daniel observed this period of special religious exercise in anticipation of the revelatory experience that came. For one thing, it was the regular passover season (cf. v. 4 with Lev. 23:4-8) during which all true Jews would be concerned with special fastings and other religious exercises. But the affairs of his people being in a low state, Daniel gave himself especially to prayer.

We learn a good deal here about the right kinds of fasting and abstinence. Note that asceticism was not his usual practice. It is clear that ordinarily Daniel drank the usual wines, ate the fine breads, and took proper care of his body. However, at this time Daniel made his *external* condition agree with his *internal* condition as an aid to importunity and continuity of his prayer. He was doing everything possible to let God know that he really meant business.

The language of verse 4 indicates that Daniel was "by the side of the great river, which is Hiddekel" in the flesh, rather than in spirit. In chapter 8 (v. 2) where it is clear that he was in Shushan by the River Ulai in vision, or spirit, the language is significantly different. There is not a word, as near as I can discern, to indicate that any of Daniel's experiences of this chapter were "in the spirit." Rather, he is represented as being very much "in the flesh" and as being brought to the very border of physical death because of those experiences. The things he saw, then, might therefore better be called "sights" than "visions," since visions in this book are mainly subjective experiences.

II THE DESCRIPTION OF THE REVELATION AND OF ITS EFFECT (Dan. 10:5-9)

Then I lifted up mine eyes, and looked, and behold a certain man clothed in linen, whose loins were girded with fine gold of Uphaz: his body also was like the beryl, and his face as the appearance of lightning, and his eyes as lamps of fire, and his arms and his feet like in colour to polished brass, and the voice of his words like the voice of a multitude (Dan. 10:5-6).

There is a serious problem of interpretation here. Is the "man clothed in linen" the same as the angel who later talks with him? In any case, whom did Daniel see?

There are many who think the angel who does the talking later is Gabriel, the angel of revelation in the preceding portions and that the One seen in the magnificent vision is none other than the Saviour, the Lord Jesus Christ, in his preincarnate state. Others think they are the same, and these usually think the person to be Gabriel.

In favor of identifying the first with our Lord are several matters. First, in Daniel 7:13, a clear prophecy of Christ, the Lord is described as "the Son of man"—similar to the description here in chapter 10. Second, in a parallel experience of Ezekiel, the prophet sees one who is by almost all interpreters identified as Deity, the description being again of one with "the appearance of a man" (Ezek. 1:26). Other features of Ezekiel's description are similar to many of Daniel's. Third, the similarity of the description to that which John gives of the Lord Jesus Christ in Revelation 1:12-20 is so great as to be almost identical. Fourth, He stands above the waters, set apart, whereas the angels on the banks do not dare to stand there (12:6). Finally, the angels in the vision appeal to this "man" as having superior knowledge, knowledge of the future which belongs only to God (12:6).

> And I Daniel alone saw the vision: for the men that were with me saw not the vision; but a great quaking fell upon them, so that they fled to hide themselves. Therefore I was left alone, and saw this great vision, and there remained no strength in me: for my comeliness was turned in me into corruption, and I retained no strength. Yet I heard the voice of his words: and when I heard the voice of his words, then was I in a deep sleep on my face, and my face toward the ground (Dan. 10:7-9).

The fact that only Daniel saw the vision and that the men with him, though conscious that something unusual was taking place, saw nothing, is another feature in common with other appearances of the exalted Christ.

This part of the story is proof also that all the events of Daniel's experiences here were in the natural waking state, not a vision in the usual sense of the word. That the sight given was supernatural is certain, of course. But the other men present were also aware of the presence of something unusual; they participated in a very reduced way in the experience. If it be objected that Daniel calls the experience a "vision," it may be answered that the word is used in Scripture for almost any kind of sight or experience. Context must determine the meaning. The context here makes it clear that Daniel saw with the organs of natural sight, his physical eyes.

"... *my comeliness was turned in me into corruption*" (Dan. 10:8). The comeliness of Daniel was his natural beauty as a living being with "appropriate strength and grace." "Corruption" might better be "disfigurement"—a related Hebrew word being used in Isaiah 52:14 of the effect of the pains of crucifixion upon our Lord.

There are some important practical truths to learn here also. Daniel did not experience any indescribable joy when as a man in the flesh he was brought into the glory-presence of God. Rather, says he, "there remained no strength in me: for my comeliness was turned into corruption, and I retained no strength." He later makes it plain that except for the strengthening of the Lord he would have died.

III. THE STRENGTHENING OF THE PROPHET TO RECEIVE A MESSAGE (Dan. 10:10-12, 15-19)

And, behold, an hand touched me, which set me upon my knees and upon the palms of my hands. And he said unto me, O Daniel, a man greatly beloved, understand the words that I speak unto thee, and stand upright: for unto thee am I now sent. And when he had spoken this word unto me, I stood trembling. Then said he unto me, Fear not, Daniel: for from the first day that thou didst set thine heart to understand, and to chasten thyself before thy God, thy words were heard, and I am come for thy words (Dan. 10:10-12).

After the initial blinding flash of the presence of the Lord and the sound of His thunderous voice Daniel lay prostrate on his face. Then shortly a hand touched him. I am inclined to believe, as asserted earlier, that the hand was the hand of another than the "man clothed in linen" (v. 5) whom we have identified with the Lord. Rather, this is one "sent" by the Lord (v. 11), and who appears to have been associated with Michael as another angel (cf. v. 21), and with still "other" angels (Dan. 12:5) who are in turn distinct from the "man clothed in linen" (Dan. 12:6).

> And when he had spoken such words unto me, I set my face toward the ground, and I became dumb. And, behold, one like the similitude of the sons of men touched my lips: then I . . . spake, and said unto him that stood before me, O my Lord, by the vision my sorrows are turned upon me, and I have retained no strength. For how can the servant of this my lord talk with this my lord? For as for me, straightway there remained no strength in me, neither is there breath left in me. Then there came again and touched me one like the appearance of a man, and he strengthened me, and said, O man greatly beloved, fear not: peace be unto thee, be strong, yea, be strong. And when he had spoken unto me, I was strengthened, and said, Let my lord speak; for thou hast strengthened me (Dan. 10:15-19).

The observing reader will have already noticed two stages in Daniel's recovery from his initial shock and fright. The touch of the angel had caused him first to rise from a completely recumbent position, face downward, to his hands and knees (v. 10). After further words of comfort he gained strength to stand "trembling" (v. 11). But as the angel continued to speak, his face drooped downward and he "became dumb" (v. 15). But a prophet must not be dumb. So the angel touched his mouth and restored his powers of speech (v. 16). But even with the power of speech restored, the overwhelmed and aged prophet had neither strength (v. 16) nor breath (v. 17) to carry on. Therefore, again the angel spoke consoling words imparting strength for the prophet to "carry on" (vv. 18-19).

IV. THE SCOPE OF THE PROPHECY (Dan. 10:14)

Now I am come to make thee understand what shall befall thy people in the latter days: for yet the vision is for many days. (Dan. 10:14).

In connection with our study of Daniel 2:28 some attention was given to the meaning of "the latter days." It is a term for the future as *consummated* with the coming of Messiah. As seen from our perspective this reaches to His second advent. This particular prophecy (Dan. 12:1-3) includes the prediction of the resurrection of the dead, final judgment, and rewards. So, in a real sense, "the latter days" is an eschatological term; but since it also includes the interval leading up to eschatological events, it is not exclusively so (see 8:26).

"The vision is for many days" indicates that Daniel was to expect that much time would elapse before the prophecy should be fulfilled.

These things being true, the final prophecy of the book may be expected to contain many things concerning God's plans for the future. Our expectation will not be disappointed, for our final study-portion, Daniel 11:36 to the end of the book, deals exclusively with eschatological matters.

But a limitation is included in the angel's words. It is not the world's future which is the subject of the prophecy, but Israel's future—"what shall befall *thy people.*" Daniel's people were the Jews. This portion of Daniel should be interpreted, in harmony with the angel's instructions, in relation to God's people Israel.

V. THE CONFLICTS OF THE ANGELIC MESSENGER (Dan. 10:13, 20-21)

But the prince of the kingdom of Persia withstood me one and twenty days: but, lo, Michael, one of the chief princes, came to help me; and I remained there with the kings of Persia. . . . Then said he, knowest thou wherefore I come unto thee? and how will I return to fight with the prince of Persia: and when I am gone forth, lo, the prince of Grecia shall come. But I will shew thee that which is noted in the scripture of truth: and there is none that holdeth with me in these things, but Michael your prince (Dan. 10:13, 20-21).

The Scripture declares that we must beware of the "wiles of the devil." Then more specifically it is said, "For we wrestle not against flesh and blood [that is, merely human opponents] but against principalities, against powers, against the rulers of the darkness of this world, against spiritual wickedness in high places" (Eph. 6:11-12). The Bible never really opens the door widely on this subject—just a gleam of light here and there. These three verses are among the clearest, though there is difficulty of interpretation.

"That which is noted in the scripture of truth" (Dan. 10:21). Though some suppose this to be the Holy Scriptures, the Bible, it seems more likely that this is a figurative expression for the decrees of God. Books appear in a number of Old Testament figures of speech and prophetic symbols (Mal. 3:16; Ps. 139:16; Ezek. 3:1 and following).

Although there are interpreters who think that the princes referred to here are the human kings of the countries named, it is the concensus of opinion that they are evil angelic spirits. Daniel had already referred to good angels as "watchers" and "holy ones" in previous chapters.

The Old Testament world was one in which men believed that each nation had its special god. The king of Nineveh called Nisroch *"his* god" (Isa. 37:38); Nebuchadnezzar named Daniel Belteshazzar "according to the name of *my* god" (Dan. 4:8). So strong was this belief that even an apostate Jewish king transferred his worship to that of his conqueror in hope of obtaining his aid (2 Chron. 28:23). And, though the idols which represented them are everywhere in Scripture declared to be vain, nothing, no breath in them, and so forth, there is also occasional information to the effect that evil spirits, not identical with the gods of the idols, were behind the whole delusion and gaining pleasure from them. It is in complete harmony with Scripture to suppose that the princes of Persia and of Greece who opposed

Gabriel were the devil's own angels (cf. Jude 9; Rev. 12:7; Matt. 25:41).

It is important to observe that Michael is mentioned as a defender, with Gabriel, of Daniel's people. In Daniel 12:1 it is said that Michael is "the great prince which standeth for the children of thy people." In the Book of Revelation a great war between Michael and his angels and the dragon and his angels is described (Rev. 12:7, and following).

May this not explain some of the mysteries of the affairs of men? The world is Satan's. He claims it, even declaring his claim in the presence of our Lord (Luke 4:5-7). He is the world's god (2 Cor. 4:4) and a prince now working in the hearts of all the unsaved (Eph. 2:2). The world lies in his control and reflects his character (1 John 5:19, John 8:44).

Since Christians wrestle against this demonical array we understand why our weapons are not of flesh (cf. 2 Cor. 10:3-4). We also understand why the leaders of our nation need our prayers, and why our chief national defences are not in military array (cf. 1 Tim. 2:1-4).

VI. PROPHECY OF THE IMMEDIATE FUTURE OF ISRAEL IN RELATION TO THE NATIONS (Dan. 11:1-35)

The 35 verses which lie before us relate to matters which are now long past. Two verses are devoted to the fortunes of ancient Medo-Persia and its kings. Two verses are devoted to the rise and fall of the great Grecian king, Alexander. The rest is all about the history of the two divisions of Alexander's empire which lay nearest Palestine, one to its south and the other to its north.

"The king of the south" is the land of Egypt and its kings of the dynasty of Ptolemy, one of Alexander's generals who inherited that part of the empire. "The king of the north" is the land of Syria and its kings of the dynasty of Seleucus, another of Alexander's generals. The Syrian kingdom came to an end when the Roman general Pompei conquered it for Rome, 63 B.C. It is of more than usual interest that the last of the so-called "kings of the south" was a queen. Her name? Cleopatra, the woman of easy morals whose amourous relations with the Roman generals Anthony and Julius Caesar are sufficiently celebrated.

This section has much in common with chapter 8. As there, the narrative moves swiftly until it reaches the time of Antiochus Epiphanes. And, as in chapter 8, the climax is a prophecy of the infamous act of that wicked and oppressive king in desecrating the Jewish temple.

A. Prophecy of the Medes and Persians (Dan. 11:1-2).

> Also in the first year of Darius the Mede, even I, stood to confirm and to strengthen him. And now will I shew thee the truth. Behold, there shall stand up yet three kings in Persia; and the fourth shall be far richer than they all: and by his strength through his riches he shall stir up against the realm of Grecia (Dan. 11:1-2).

We may only surmise the purpose of the angelic strengthening of Darius in his first year. His first year as vassal-king of Babylon apparently coincides with Cyrus' first year. Perhaps it had something to do with the kind treatment both of these kings (except for the unfortunate incident of chapter 6) accorded the Jews. It was Cyrus who at this time granted the Jews permission to return home to Palestine and furnish resources for the return. We now know from archaeology that this generosity was part of a general policy of Cyrus toward the uprooted peoples of the Babylonian period.

The rest is familiar to all students of ancient history. Cyrus, the first king of the Empire of the Persians, was on the throne at the time of Daniel's experience. The second was an imposter—called Pseudo-Smerdis by the historians. Next came a truly great king, Darius Hystaspis, the man who began serious planning for the conquest of Europe. The fourth, Darius' son Xerxes, the Ahasuerus of the Book of Esther. Nothing is said of Xerxes' successors.

B. Prophecy of the Greeks and of Alexander (Dan. 11:3-4). It is not necessary to repeat here what has already been said about these things in connection with chapters 7 and 8.

C. Prophecy concerning Syria and Egypt, the historic kings of the north and of the south, in conflict with one another and with the Jews (vv. 5-35).

It is neither feasible nor profitable in the present exposition to trace the correspondence between Daniel's prophecy of these two kingdoms and the history of the period. The prophecy does not cover every section of the period, that is to say, there are gaps in the coverage. Neither is present knowledge of the period sufficiently complete to give a full picture.

A helpful confirmation of the Danielic authorship and early date of the book is to be found here. Egypt is mentioned by name, in such a way as to indicate that it is the king of the south (v. 8, cf. v. 9), but the kingdom of the Seleucids, called the king of the north is unnamed. We refer to it as Syria, but really that is inaccurate inasmuch as the territory of this dynasty included much more than the geographical area known as Syria, and was unrelated to the Old Testament kingdom of that name. This appears to be because though Egypt was known in the time of Daniel in the sixth century, being a very ancient nation, the kingdom of the Seleucids was not yet in existence and mention of its name would have been meaningless.

It is at verse 21 that the prophecy becomes most significant, for here Antiochus Epiphanes (see notes concerning him in comments on chapter 8), the wicked persecutor of the Jews in the second century B.C. is introduced as "a vile person." This is the man who introduced vile pagan worship in the temple, known to the prophet at Daniel 8:13 as "the transgression of desolation" and here at verse 31 as "the abomination that maketh desolate." There is similar language used at Daniel 9:27, "for the overspreading of abominations he shall make it desolate" in prediction of a future desecration of a restored Jewish temple in the times of the coming Antichrist. Jesus' reference to "the abomination of desolation ... spoken of through Daniel the prophet" is to Daniel 9:27 and 12:11, not to Daniel 8:13 and 11:31. It is clear that Jesus was thinking of an act of complete desecration still future in His own time, predicting that it would occur in times just before His second coming, and warning His disciples against it (Matt. 24:15-21). The prophecies of the sufferings of Israel under Antiochus were to take place within the Old Testament epoch, though some centuries in the future at the time Daniel wrote.

In the days of Antiochus only those who knew "their God" (v. 32) were able to hold up their heads without shame. It was they who were helped by God, being enabled to "do exploits" (v. 32). The Apocryphal books of Maccabees tell the details of their heroism and Hebrews 11:34-39 memorializes them as heroes of faith. Many of them were to die for their faith (vv. 34-35), but their lives were to teach others (v. 33) and their sufferings were to make them pure, by the help of God (vv. 34-35).

These godly heroes of the 160s and 150s B.C. were the separatists of their day. They believed in being separate from the pagan vices of the Greeks and from the lies of the pagan religion and its attractive ritual. They are the main link between Old and New Testaments, for the spiritual descendants of these people who appear in prediction in the Old Testament appear on the pages of our Gospels as the Pharisees—the name means "separated ones." It is sad to know that many of them fell far from their original principles.

12

Daniel 11:36–12:13

Summary of Old Testament Eschatology:

Israel's Final Future in the Plan of God

I. The Prophecy Concerning the Future "Willful King" (Dan. 11:36-45)

II. Prophecy Concerning the Great Tribulation of Israel (Dan. 12:1)

III. Prophecy Concerning the Resurrection of the Dead (Dan. 12:2)

IV. Prophecy Concerning the Final Reward of the Righteous (Dan. 12:3)

V. Final Prophecies and Instructions (Dan. 12:4-13)

Though effort has been made to avoid using the technical term, "eschatology," and its relative, "eschatological," it has appeared a few times in these studies, and there it now stands in the title of this last study in Daniel. So it must be defined. Almost all of the technical terms of theology come from the ancient Greek language. This is because the early Christian theologians spoke and wrote in Greek. "Theology," itself, is one of those terms. Now, the common Greek word for "last" or "last thing" is *eschatos* (pronounded es-ka-tos). The Greek word for a treatise, word, or discussion is *logos*. Put the two words together and with a bit of abbreviation and the addition of an English word-ending the result is "eschatology," the study of last things. These topics are firstly those relating to the ultimate future of men personally, such as death, the intermediate state between death and resurrection, resurrection, judgment, heaven, hell, and so forth. They are, secondly, matters relating to the future of the human race, such as the Second Coming of Christ, the Great Tribulation, the Antichrist, and so forth.

Inasmuch as the whole Bible is related to man's ultimate destiny, designed by God to lead men into eternal life, it is all eschatological in a general way. Yet, inasmuch as these last portions of the Book of Daniel relate specifically to technically eschatological questions, it is eschatology in a narrow sense. Light on a number of questions and topics only slightly treated in earlier portions of the Bible is here brightened. Information on some others is here for the first time clearly introduced.

I PROPHECY CONCERNING THE FUTURE "WILLFUL KING" (Dan. 11:36-45)

Somewhere in this prophecy between the end of verse 4 of chapter 11 and the opening of chapter 12 the prediction shifts from the historic kingdoms of antiquity to "last things." Interpreters are generally agreed in this, but they greatly disagree as to just where the break comes.

As indicated by my expository divisions it is my opinion

that the break comes between verses 35 and 36. If the student has carefully read chapters 11 and 12, the following summary of arguments should be sufficient to demonstrate that this division is at least feasible. A fact strongly in favor of this view is that a majority of reverent scholars have favored it. Jerome states that this portion was applied to Antichrist by "our writers" in his day, and he, himself, favored the interpretation.

A. The scope of the prophecy, as indicated by the words of Gabriel (10:14) demands eschatological prophecy somewhere in this part of Daniel, for he said that it was for "the latter days." This alone makes our view a possibility.

B. All of chapter 11, down to verse 35, can be shown to relate to rather well-known events of the ancient history of Syria and Egypt. It is quite impossible to find such correspondence between any known events of antiquity and 11:36-45. It is logical then to suppose these verses refer to some other period.

C. The mention in verse 36 of a king who "shall prosper till the indignation be accomplished" suggests end-times. "The indignation" is a technical term out of the predictive literature of the Old Testament usually having an end-time setting. See Isaiah 26:20 for an illustrative passage.

D. Of much greater weight is the fact that this section contains predictions which correspond quite precisely with many other unquestionable predictions of the coming Antichrist. See especially the second chapter of 2 Thessalonians and chapters 13 and 17 of Revelation. This outlook has the support of most recent evangelical writers.

E. For those sufficiently interested to give the passage thorough study, it will be important to note that there is a natural break in thought at verse 36, a break observed by the paragraphing of several versions and translations.

F. Though not of decisive force, the phrase, "at the time of the end" (11:40) supports our view; that is, that the transition to eschatology has been passed.

G. Of decisive force, in my opinion, is the connection indicated between chapters 11 and 12. Chapter 12 begins, "And at that time." There follow the Great Tribulation, the resurrection of the dead, and the final reward of the righteous—certainly eschatological. So the last part of chapter 11, at least, is eschatological—for it is "at the same time.' This is of decisive importance. The best place to make the break before the beginning of chapter 12 is between verses 35 and 36, for here is introduced a new king. This king does "according to his will" and seems to be neither the king of the north nor the king of the south who are being discussed in the preceding section.

> And the king shall do according to his will; and he shall exalt himself, and magnify himself above every god, and shall speak marvellous things against the God of gods, and shall prosper till the indignation be accomplished: for that is determined shall be done (Dan. 11:36).

This is the same as the "son of perdition" referred to in 2 Thessalonians, where it is said that as "man of sin" he "opposeth and exalteth himself above all that is called God, of that is worshipped; so that he sitteth in the temple of God, shewing himself that he is God" (2 Thess. 2:3-4). Paul places his appearing just before our Saviour's own second coming (2 Thess. 2:8-9). The actions of this "man of sin" are the same as those ascribed to him under the figure of the "little horn" in chapter 7: "He shall speak great words against the most High" (Dan. 7:25 cf. 7:11). Antiochus, as his type, was to portray some of these characteristics, for "he magnified himself even to the prince of the host. . . . He shall also stand up against the Prince of princes" (8:11, 25).

But his career shall be short—only till the "indignation be accomplished"—till the brief time of three and one-half years (Dan. 7:25; 9:27; Rev. 17:10, 17; 13:5) during which God shall use him to judge wicked men.

> Neither shall he regard the God of his fathers, nor the desire of women, nor regard any god: for he shall magnify himself above all (Dan. 11:37).

An interesting touch is added here. If he is to be an anti-Christ, he will be a Jew, for the word "anti" in Greek means "instead of" rather than "opposed to." If he is to pose for a while as the Jewish Christ (Messiah) it would appear necessary for him to be a Jew. The "God of his fathers" is, then, the Jehovah God of Israel. Some modern translations render the passage "gods of his fathers." But the many scriptural references to the "God of your fathers," or the "God of their fathers," or "Lord God," and others, make it close to a certainty that the common expression for the Jewish God, Jehovah, is meant here. Besides, no true Jew will ever accept a known pagan as his Christ. At first, he will appear to be a pious Jew. Afterward his true character will come to light.

"Nor the desire of women" has been variously interpreted to mean anything from certain womanly idols to sexual interest. The exact meaning is still unknown. Since in the next verse the wicked king is represented as honoring another, this is evidence that it is a reference to the Antichrist. Jerome observes that in his day some thought the phrase meant that Antichrist would make a show of chastity, that he had no lust for women. Yet Jerome's own translation of the passage indicates that he felt it should read "he shall be engrossed in lust for women."

> But in his estate shall he honour the God of forces: and a god whom his fathers knew not shall he honour with gold, and silver, and with precious stones, and pleasant things. Thus shall he do in the most strong holds with a strange god, whom he shall acknowledge and increase with glory: and he shall cause them to rule over many, and shall divide the land for gain (Dan. 11:38-39).

A better rendering of "but in his estate he shall honor the God of forces" might be: "But in its place he shall honor the god of force." In other words, the Antichrist shall make the winning of wars his god—"Might makes right."

Not very long ago the people of Germany had a ruler known about the world as Adolph Hitler. He rejected the Christian God of the official churches of the land. Openly he claimed to honor the state of Germany, itself, as his god, suggesting that he himself, as its head, was a sort of god He resurrected the pre-Christian deities of the German tribes. But secretly he practiced astrology and consulted fortune-tellers and other practitioners of the occult arts.

This appears to be the kind of man the willful king of this chapter will be. While proclaiming himself as a god, and honoring "forces" (military power, perhaps) above everything else, he will be inwardly a spiritual quack, practicing the most foolish things.

The climax of his career in the momentous events leading to his end at the very appearing of the Lord Jesus Christ to judge and rule the nations, and to deliver his ancient people Israel, is described in the next five verses. It is "at the time of the end" (v. 40). Paul tells us "then shall that Wicked be revealed, whom the Lord shall consume with the spirit of his mouth, and shall destroy with the brightness of his coming" (2 Thess. 2:8-9). Isaiah 11:4 describes the same events as does also Revelation 19:11 and following. The twelfth and fourteenth chapters of Zechariah give the locale and time of these events. Israel, returned to their land in unbelief, shall be attacked by this man's forces. They shall be hopelessly outnumbered and overpowered but shall be delivered by the appearing of the very Son of God, their Messiah. This will be followed by the Millennium. The six verses before us portray the growing complex of affairs in the career of the willful king, the man of sin, leading up to that consummation.

> And at the time of the end shall the king of the south push at him: and the king of the north shall come against him like a whirlwind, with chariots, and with horsemen, and with many ships; and he shall enter into the countries, and shall overflow and pass over (Dan. 11:40).

The willful king will be successful at war. Having appeared on the scene of world affairs as a little horn, he shall begin his conquests by rudely toppling the crowns from off the heads of three neighboring kings (cf. Dan. 7:8, 20). Toward the end this king shall grow in power rapidly till all the "horns" with "one mind" shall give their power and strength unto the beast" (Rev. 17:13). But others will remain opposed to him. Among these appear to be the king of the south (Egypt) and the king of the north (Syria). Incidentally the willful king of these verses cannot be Antiochus Epiphanes for he was a king of the north. Despite the fierceness of their attack with all kinds of weapons and forces (for that must be the meaning of "whirlwind ... chariots ... horsemen ... ships")—the willful king shall win.

> He shall enter also into the glorious land, and many countries [countries is not in the Hebrew] shall be overthrown: but these shall escape out of his hand, even Edom, and Moab, and the chief of the children of Ammon (Dan. 11:41).

Although much of this must await the fulfillments for exposition, one thing is clear, this king will invade the Holy Land (for such is the obvious meaning of "the glorious land" to the expatriated old patriarch who wrote the words) but without complete success. Many people, presumably of that "glorious land" shall be overthrown, but not all. "It is interesting to observe how these three districts, of which at this time he does not take possession, are specified in Isaiah 11:14 as falling into the hands of restored Israel—'they shall lay their hand upon Edom and Moab; and the children of Ammon shall obey them' " (S. P. Tregelles).

> He shall stretch forth his hand also upon the countries: and the land of Egypt shall not escape. But he shall have power over the treasures of gold and of silver, and over all the precious things of Egypt: and the Libyans and the Ethiopians shall be at his steps. But tidings out of the east and out of the north shall trouble him: therefore he shall go forth with great fury to destroy, and utterly to make away many (Dan. 11:42-44).

Some readers will remember that in the 1930s, when World War II was shaping up, this was a very popular section of the Bible for sermons on prophecy, especially these verses. The Russians were beginning to look big on the international horizon; Hitler was just becoming well known.

The British were still the leading European power. But the really startling customer was Benito Mussolini, premier of Italy. He had galvanized his own Italy into something of a first-class country again, had built up what looked like a fair army, had talked boastfully and loudly of a revival of the traditions of the Caesars in Italy, and had boldly set out to restore the Roman Empire of old. Was he the "little horn"? If so, then we might look for him soon to pluck up three other kingdoms and begin his march to power.

With the passage of the years in those fateful thirties the correspondence of certain events of international history with these verses became so startlingly close that not a few declared that the final lineup of nations for Armageddon was taking place before our very eyes. The willful king of verse 36 who exalted himself above every god (which Mussolini really did), and boasted and bragged of his own greatness (v. 37), and who worshiped Mars, the god of war (v. 38), was convincingly declared by many to be Mussolini. The king of the south (v. 40), on what seemed to be pretty good grounds, was identified with the British Empire (at that time ruling Egypt, the old-time king of the south). The king of the north was thought to be an alliance of the two northern countries, Germany and Russia (Ezek. 38 was usually read at this point). When the non-aggression agreement between Hitler and Stalin was effected in 1939 this interpretation was in its heyday. In the mid-thirties Mussolini took over large sections of Africa, including Libya and Ethiopia. Didn't Daniel write (v. 43) that the "Libyians and the Ethiopians shall be at his steps"? The accumulation of evidence was simply astounding.

But, alas, in less than ten years poor Mussolini was strung by his heels, naked and dead, from the front shed of a gasoline station; Hitler and Stalin had broken their pact and had fought one another in a deadly war ruining many a sermon on Ezekiel 38. The British Empire had well-nigh passed away spoiling the sermons on Daniel 11:42-44, and the prophetic preachers had simply changed the subject. The preaching of prophecy simply died out. But, sad to say, along with it much of the old-time emphasis on and interest in the coming of our Lord and the light which the Bible sheds on related things partly died out too. Having learned only too well that "prophecy was not given in order that we should prophesy"; we ought to revive our interest in the things that lead us to watch more earnestly and hopefully for the coming again of the Son of Man. This should be without yielding to the temptations of sensationalism.

There is quite a list here of countries among the ancient neighbors of the Jews. Daniel 11:41–"but these shall escape out of his hand, even Edom, and Moab, and the chief of the children of Ammon." Daniel 11:43–"The Libyans and the Ethiopians shall be at his steps." In addition Palestine itself is mentioned in the context as "the glorious land" (v. 41). Other lands of the "east and . . . the north" appear (v. 44). These become very difficult of interpretation for those who do not expect Israel ever to return to their land, and who expect no literal reign of Christ and His saints over the earth in a future Millennium. Yet some of these Bible-honoring interpreters feel that the Antichrist is a real person of the last days. They find it hard to make sense of a passage with a real Antichrist but only figurative enemies for him. I think this method of interpretation lacks biblical authority. Incidentally, prophecies in Isaiah, Jeremiah and Ezekiel predict restoration for several of these lands "in the latter days."

> And he shall plant the tabernacles of his palace between the seas in the glorious holy mountain; yet he shall come to his end, and none shall help him (Dan. 11:45).

Having moved to Palestine with his troops to put an end to the hated Jewish people, the Antichrist will plant the "tabernacles of his palace," that is, his royal pavilions, between the seas, possibly the Dead Sea and the Mediterranean Sea in the neighborhood of the holy mount on which sits the ancient Holy City of Jerusalem. There he will feel the blast of God which will spell his end (cf. Joel 3:16).

This moment of the eternal ruin of Satan's man of sin is of

great interest to the writers of the Bible. The Holy Spirit of prophecy has imparted a good deal about it. The enterprising students will find some of these materials in the twelfth and fourteenth chapters of Zechariah, the third chapter of Joel, Revelation 14:17-20 and chapter 19.

In his final end, being destroyed by the direct action of God Almighty, without ordinary human hands, Antiochus' death of grief in Babylon may be regarded as a type.

II. PROPHECY CONCERNING THE GREAT TRIBULATION OF ISRAEL (Dan. 12:1)

And at that time shall Michael stand up, the great prince which standeth for the children of thy people: and there shall be a time of trouble, such as never was since there was a nation even to that same time: and at that time thy people shall be delivered, every one that shall be found written in the book (Dan. 12:1).

Michael is the great angelic defender of Israel, according to these words. When we are told in Revelation 12:7 that there is celestial warfare in which Michael and his angels fight we are not to dismiss this as mere poetic language. Angels appear often in the biblical story as defenders of Israel. A great angelic being appeared to Joshua as "captain of the Lord's host" to give assurance to that embattled leader just before the conquest of Jericho (Joshua 5:13-15). It was "the angel of the Lord" that destroyed 180,000 Assyrians in a single night when they were encamped against Jerusalem (Isa. 37:35-36).

The "time of trouble, such as never was since there was a nation even to that same time" is the short period of time near the end of this age commonly known as the Great Tribulation. But, whatever may be said about the period elsewhere, the interest of Daniel in it is that his people, Israel, shall suffer during it. Jeremiah also speaks at length of this period. He speaks of it as a day when men shall be in pain like that of women in childbirth (Jer. 30:4-6). Jeremiah makes clear the purpose of it as a kind of final chastening of Israel by the Lord before He permanently and finally resumes His special relationship with them.

Several passages speak of this time as a period of "indignation" during which all men living on the earth shall suffer greatly. Both Isaiah 26:20 and Daniel 11:36 speak of it in this way. Many passages in Revelation, which apparently describe these things in detail, speak of the suffering of men in general. Wars, pestilences, great fires, unnatural and supernatural afflictions of various sorts, until it is said "they gnawed their tongues for pain" (Rev. 16:10) shall prevail.

Israel, however, will emerge triumphant and glorious out of it. "It is even the time of Jacob's trouble; but he shall be saved out of it" (Jer. 30:7).

A question which many today find important is: Will there be Christian believers on earth during those days, or will the Lord remove them by a "rapture" beforehand? It is a question which all might wish had been given a more direct answer by the Lord, for there is the utmost diversity of opinion about it.

The post-tribulationists expect the church to remain on earth till the very end, anticipating no "rapture" before the tribulation. They point out that 2 Thessalonians 2:1 and following appears to place the revelation of the man of sin before the Second Coming of Christ, especially inasmuch as "our gathering together unto him," and the "coming of our Lord Jesus Christ" (v. 1) and "the day of Christ" (v. 2) appear to be used as synonyms for the second coming event. If the revelation of the man of sin is to precede the gathering of the saints together to Christ, then they will be here through the tribulation.

A small, but apparently growing, number affirm that the rapture will be mid-seventieth week but pre-tribulational. Arguments are based on the order of events in the Olivet discourse of Jesus as compared with Revelation 4-19, the alleged connection of the last trumpet of the seven in Revelation and the "last trumpet" of 1 Thessalonians 4:13-18. Others find support for a rapture in the midst of the week but before the "wrath" of God in the vials of Revelation by arguing from the two harvests of Revelation 14:14-20. The first is of wheat (believers); the latter one of grapes (unbelievers).

Those who see the "rapture" of the Church before the tribulation (pre-tribulationists) cite such passages as 1 Thessalonians 1:10; 5:9; Revelation 3:10. A very strong argument for this view is the fact that between Revelation 3:22 and 4:1 there is a definite break in setting and participants. After Revelation 3:22 there is no longer a mention of the Church, the Body of Christ, until Revelation 22:16. These Scriptures and similar passages are used to support the view that the "rapture" takes place before the beginning of the seventieth week of Daniel. This is the view set forth in the Scofield Bible and is by far the most common view among premillennialists of recent generations.

III. PROPHECY CONCERNING THE RESURRECTION OF THE DEAD (Dan. 12:2)

And many of them that sleep in the dust of the earth shall awake, some to everlasting life, and some to shame and everlasting contempt" (Dan. 12:2).

This verse, like the rest of the prophecy, relates especially to the Israelites.

It is probably true that if this verse were the only one in the Bible on the subject of the resurrection of the dead, most readers would feel there is to be but one future resurrection— a general resurrection in which all, both righteous and unrighteous, would participate. But this verse is only the first of a long series of passages relating to the resurrection of the dead. Others which at least suggest two future resurrections, one of the righteous and another of the unrighteous, are John 5:28-29 and Acts 24:15. First Corinthians 15:20-24 states that all men shall sometime be raised from the dead. They will be in several groups. Christ the firstfruits is a group by Himself; the righteous in Christ are another group "at his coming"; the rest presumably will be raised at "the end," that is, an end resurrection. Revelation 20:1-7 shows that there is to be a "first resurrection" followed by the Millennium when the saints shall reign on earth with Christ, and after which the resurrection of the wicked dead shall take place—"after the thousand years are finished."

In support of the premillennial view advocated here is the translation suggested by S. P. Teegelles, a German author named Gerhard Kerkherdere, and by the Jewish scholars Saadiah Haggaon (tenth century) and Aben Ezra (twelfth century). It reads: "And many from among the sleepers of the dust of the earth shall awake; these shall be unto everlasting life; but those [the rest of the sleepers, those who do not awake at this time] shall be unto shame and everlasting contempt." This translation may be sustained by the Hebrew text and is presented here as being, in this writer's opinion, the correct one.

IV. PROPHECY CONCERNING THE FINAL REWARD OF THE RIGHTEOUS (Dan. 12:3)

> And they that be wise shall shine as the brightness of the firmament; and they that turn many to righteousness as the stars for ever and ever (Dan. 12:3).

Who are these "wise" (Heb. *wise ones*)? The same word appears in the Hebrew Bible at 11:33 where it is translated "they that understand," and at 11:35 where it is translated "them of understanding." It appears again in chapter 12, verse 10, where it is translated "the wise." In chapter 11 the two references are to the loyal people of Israel who, understanding and believing God's Word, stood up under the trials and persecutions of Antiochus Epiphanes. The wise of Daniel 12:3, the verse before us, as well as in verse 10, are saints of the end-time (see Mal. 3:16-17 and context). But the principles involved apply to people of all ages.

What does it mean to "shine as the brightness of the firmament . . . as the stars for ever and ever"?

> Daniel's Jewish training had taught him how to purge and elevate these conceptions: that "firmament" was God's creation (Gen. 1:6; Ps. 19:1); its "brightness" a testimony to His greatness

(Exod. 24:10) the "stars" were of God's ordinance, their number "told" by Him, their names "called" by Him; "in their courses they fought" against His enemies and "made obeisance to" His servants (Ps. 8:3; Gen. 1:16; Ps. 147:4; Judges 5:20; Gen. 37:9). The words of Daniel were afterwards applied by our Lord Himself to the "righteous" (Matt. 13:43), and the imagery became sanctified to Christian use (1 Cor. 15:40; Rev. 2:28) (J. M. Fuller).

V. FINAL PROPHECIES AND INSTRUCTIONS (Dan. 12:4-13)

1. The Disposition of the Book.

But thou, O Daniel, shut up the words, and seal the book, even to the time of the end: many shall run to and fro, and knowledge shall be increased (Dan. 12:4).

These words have to do with the preservation and the understanding of the prophecies of Daniel.

The Old Testament has quite a lot to say about the sealing of books—all relating to their authentication as being genuinely written by the parties whose names and signatures they bear and to their preservation until the proper parties might open and read them. As far as we can see, nothing about obscuration of the meaning (as some assert) until any certain time is involved in sealing. The fact that we still have Daniel's book, in the original languages and in the many translations, is the fulfillment of the purpose of sealing.

The latter half of the verse has no reference at all to increased facility of travel in modern times (steamships, railroads, automobiles, airplanes, and so forth). Neither does it refer to the advances in scientific knowledge. Leupold's rendering gives the right meaning: "Many shall diligently peruse it, and knowledge shall be increased." The running to and fro is of the eyes of the diligent readers on the page of the book of prophecy as down through the years God's people have read this book, and other books of Scripture. As the centuries roll on our understanding of all the Bible grows.

2. Lord! How Long?

Then I Daniel looked, and, behold, there stood other two, the one on this side of the bank of the river, and the other on that side of the bank of the river. And one said to the man clothed in linen, which was upon the waters of the river, how long shall it be to the end of these wonders? And I heard the man clothed in linen, which was upon the waters of the river, when he held up his right hand and his left hand unto heaven, and sware by him that liveth for ever that it shall be for a time, times, and a half; and when he shall have accomplished to scatter the power of the holy people, all these things shall be finished (Dan. 12:5-7).

The manner of oath-taking seen here is most impressive: "... he held up his right hand and his left hand unto heaven, and sware by him that liveth for ever that it should be." With regard to this oath "Abram said to the king of Sodom, I have lift up mine hand unto the Lord, the most high God" (Gen. 14:22). In Deuteronomy 32:40 God Himself is represented as lifting up His hand to heaven in making an oath. So the lifting of the right hand along with making an affirmation were features of oath-taking. The raising of both hands, as here, presumably was to render the statement even more affirmative.

One day after the risen Christ had been speaking of His kingdom with His apostles (Acts 1:6), and they were all together for the very last time, "they asked of him, saying, Lord wilt thou at this time restore again the kingdom to Israel?" His answer was simply that it was not for them to know the "times or the seasons." There was not a word of correction about their persistent expectation of a future special kingdom for the Jews. There was, however, instruction concerning what to do in the meantime.

Daniel was in a position similar to that of the Apostles. The days of special revelations were at an end. Even the angels present with Daniel did not know just when the momentous events predicted would take place. One of them asked the man clothed with linen (the Son of God) who was "above the waters of the river" (Dan. 12:6 ASV), "How long shall it be to the end of these wonders?" The angel addressed the right party, for only an omnipotent God knows the future.

The answer in effect was first to give a solemn oath that what revelation had already been imported in this and previous revelations was absolutely true, and then to say no more, merely calling upon the interested parties to study further the "time, times, and an half" already mentioned in previous prophecies. Both the oath and the instruction are useful for us today. If life is to go on with joy and with courage we have to know that things are coming out right, at the end, according to God's oath. God is the "end of the line" in our human search for certainty. "For . . . God . . . , because he could swear by no greater, he sware by himself" (Heb. 6:13). God, Himself, in Christ is our sufficient hope.

The direction to study what has already been written, seeking no further special revelations but to study and wait applies directly to men today. In our day of a "silent heaven," when "there is no more any prophet: neither is there among us any that knoweth how long" (Ps. 74:9); we must be satisfied that "whatsoever things were written aforetime were written for our learning, that we through patience and comfort of the scriptures might have hope" (Rom. 15:4).

3. What Shall the End Be Like?

> And I heard, but I understood not: then said I, O my Lord, what shall be the end of these things? And he said, Go thy way, Daniel: for the words are closed up and sealed till the time of the end. Many shall be purified, and made white, and tried; but the wicked shall do wickedly: and none of the wicked shall understand; but the wise shall understand. And from the time that the daily sacrifice shall be taken away, and the abomination that maketh desolate set up, there shall be a thousand two hundred and ninety days. Blessed is he that waiteth, and cometh to the thousand three hundred and five and thirty days (Dan. 12:8-12).

Though these words have a certain cryptic flavor, they should not be regarded as essentially impossible to interpret. The times or "things" in which Daniel, following the leading of the angel (v. 8, cf. v. 6), showed his interest, was the period of the Great Tribulation lasting three times (years) and a half. The Book of Revelation informs us that this period is to be concluded with the coming of Christ a second time, to save His people Israel, to judge and destroy Antichrist and his followers, to raise the righteous dead, and to set up the kingdom promised (Rev. 19 and 20). With all the problems some raise against such a program, it still is the succession of future events announced by the Scriptures. If this is true then the 1,260 days will finish their course at the very end of the Great Tribulation, beginning at the midpoint of the seventieth week (Dan. 9:27, cf. Rev. 11:2-3; Dan. 7:25; Matt. 24:21-22). The 1,290 days would therefore extend 30 days into the Millennium for there is no hint in Scripture of any lapse of time between the close of the seventieth week and the inauguration of Christ's millennial reign. I think we may tentatively suppose it to be a period, shall we say, of "mopping up" exercises. As to the 1,335 days, the best suggestion I know of is that passed along by Harry Ironside: "A longer period yet is given in verse 12: 'Blessed is he that waiteth, and cometh to the thousand three hundred and five and thirty days.' Some have suggested that this would carry on the time to the celebration of the first millenial feast of tabernacles, as in the fourteenth chapter of Zechariah. At any rate it clearly points us on to the full establishment of the kingdom in power and glory."

ADDITIONAL STUDY GUIDES IN THIS SERIES . . .

GENESIS, John P. Burke, $3.95.
EXODUS, Tom Julien, $3.95.
DEUTERONOMY, Bernard N. Schneider, $3.95.
JOSHUA, JUDGES & RUTH, John J. Davis, $3.95.
1 & 2 SAMUEL & 1 KINGS 1-11, John J. Davis, $3.95.
KINGS & CHRONICLES, John C. Whitcomb, $3.95.
PROVERBS, Charles W. Turner, $3.95.
MATTHEW, Harold H. Etling, $3.95.
GOSPEL OF JOHN, Homer A. Kent, Jr., $3.95.
ACTS, Homer A. Kent, Jr., $3.95.
ROMANS, Herman A. Hoyt, $3.95.
1 CORINTHIANS, James L. Boyer, $3.95.
GALATIANS, Homer A. Kent, Jr., $3.95.
EPHESIANS, Tom Julien, $3.95.
PHILIPPIANS, David L. Hocking, $3.95.
1 & 2 TIMOTHY, Dean Fetterhoff, $3.95.
HEBREWS, Herman A. Hoyt, $3.95.
JAMES, Roy R. Roberts, $3.95.
1, 2, 3 JOHN, Raymond E. Gingrich, $3.95.
REVELATION, Herman A. Hoyt, $3.95.
THE WORLD OF UNSEEN SPIRITS, Bernard N. Schneider, $3.95.
THE HOLY SPIRIT AND YOU, Bernard N. Schneider, $3.95.
PROPHECY, THINGS TO COME, James L. Boyer, $3.95.
PULPIT WORDS TRANSLATED FOR PEW PEOPLE,
   Charles W. Turner, $3.95.
SWEETER THAN HONEY, Jesse B. Deloe *(A guide to effective Bible study and the background of how we got our Bible)*, $3.95.
THE FAMILY FIRST, Kenneth O. Gangel, $2.50.

Obtain from your local Christian bookstore or by mail from BMH Books, P.O. Box 544, Winona Lake, Ind. 46590. (Include a check with your order and BMH Books pays postage.)